DELIVERING QUALITY SERVICE

◇ ◇ ◇

Balancing Customer Perceptions and Expectations

Valarie A. Zeithaml
A. Parasuraman
Leonard L. Berry

THE FREE PRESS

New York

THE FREE PRESS
A Division of Simon & Schuster Inc.
1230 Avenue of the Americas
New York, NY 10020

Manufactured in the United States of America

printing number

19   20   18

Library of Congress Cataloging-in-Publication Data

Zeithaml, Valarie A.
    Delivering quality service : balancing customer perceptions and
expectations / Valarie A. Zeithaml, A. Parasuraman, Leonard L.
Berry.
        p.   cm.
    Includes bibliographical references.
    ISBN 10: 1-4391-6728-1   ISBN 13: 978-1-4391-6728-1
    1. Customer service.   2. Service industries—Quality control—
Mathematical models.   I. Parasuraman, A.   II. Berry, Leonard L.
III. Title.
HF5415.5.Z45   1990
658.8'12—dc20   89–23592
                                                          CIP

To the Marketing Science Institute for encouraging and supporting the research stream on which this book is based.

To my father, John McKinley Hoyle,
for thinking the big thought.

—V. Z.

To my mother, and in memory of my father.

—A. P.

To Lester Gold, a special uncle,
who taught me to touch all of the bases.

—L. B.

CONTENTS

PREFACE

In 1983 WE SUBMITTED OUR FIRST PROPOSAL to the Marketing Science Institute (MSI) for funds to do an exploratory research study on the subject of service quality. Little did we know at the time that we were embarking on a research *journey* as infinite as the subject itself.

As we prepare this preface we are six months away from the new decade of the 1990's. And we are still on our research journey under the auspices of MSI, soon to do the fieldwork for phase IV. Phase I was an extensive qualitative study of service customers and service-company executives that resulted in our developing a model of service quality. Phase II was a large-scale empirical study that focused on the customer side of our service-quality model. From this phase we developed a methodology for measuring service quality that we call SERVQUAL and we refined our conclusions concerning the dimensions customers use to judge service quality.

Phase III was an empirical study that focused on the service provider half of our model and our most complex and ambitious effort to date. Phase III alone involved research in 89 separate field offices of five national service companies. The three research phases together have included customer focus-group interviews, employee focus-group interviews, in-depth executive interviews, customer surveys, manager surveys, and first-line employee surveys. We have studied six service sectors thus far: appliance repair, credit cards, insurance, long-distance telephone, retail banking and securities brokerage.

Phase IV centers on the topic of customer service expectations: how customers form their expectations and the key influences that affect this process. Our research protocol has been to explore through qualitative research, model what we find, and then test relationships within the model quantitatively. We will follow this protocol with our expectations research, doing a large number of customer focus groups in phase IV. In phase IV we will also add services we have not yet studied (automobile service, business equipment service, hotels, and truck rental) to some of the services included in the earlier phases.

In this book we present the fruits of our research journey to date. Using our model as the central framework, we seek to demonstrate that service quality is a subject that one can grab hold of, understand, and do something about. It *is* a subject that lends itself to research insight and managerial application.

From the very beginning of our research effort in 1983 we have been interested in three central questions:

- What is service quality?
- What causes service-quality problems?
- What can organizations do to solve these problems and improve their service?

With three phases of research complete, we believe we have something to say about each of these questions and we have written this book to say it. Although we have published a series of journal articles and research monographs on various facets of our research, this is our first attempt to bring everything together in one volume—our model, our methodologies, our findings, and our conclusions. We also go beyond our formal research findings and present many ideas, quotes, and company case histories that we have picked up on our journey. Having devoted a significant portion of the last seven years living the quality of service issue—reading everything we could get our hands on, talking to anyone who would talk to us, doing our formal studies, becoming the toughest of service critics in our own lives as customers—we have the patterns and nuances of our internal thoughts to share on this subject, too.

Our objectives for this book can be distilled quite simply:

- to attack head-on the mystique, mush, and myths that surround the service-quality issue and limit progress;
- to offer a framework that managers can actually use to understand and improve service quality;
- to offer specific and practical guidelines for improving service; and
- to convey the sense of urgency that we feel about improving service quality in America.

Our book is for senior and middle mangers in all types of service organizations. It is decidedly for *line* executives, not just for staff executives. Although we use the terms *company* or *firm* as a writing convenience, we believe strongly that managers in not-for-profit organizations can gain from this volume and we hope they will give it a try.

All of our formal research has been done in the United States and thus we focus on the United States as the setting for our discussion. We do not wish to imply that our findings necessarily apply to other countries as we have no empirical basis for making such an inference. We can say, however, that scholars throughout the world are using our research as a basis for their own studies, a very pleasing development that became evident to us at the International Research Seminar in Marketing held in the South of France during May 1988 and the Symposium on Quality in Services held in Karlstad, Sweden, during August 1988.

We have many people to thank who have supported our research financially and intellectually. First and foremost, we wish to express our deep appreciation to the Marketing Science Institute in Cambridge, Massachusetts, a one-of-a-kind jewel of an organization that funds leading-edge academic research of interest to its company sponsors. We know of no other research organization in America that has done more to build a bridge between the academic and business communities, and to advance marketing knowledge, than MSI.

We owe a great debt to Diane Schmalensee, head of research operations at MSI through phases I-III and the start-up of phase IV; she worked tirelessly to help us succeed in our work. Katherine Jocz, manager of research operations, has also been tremendously helpful, as have John Farley and Frederick Webster who served as MSI executive directors during our research. Alden Clayton, a past president of MSI, was very supportive of us during the crucial early days of our research journey.

Including phase IV, more than 15 major U.S. companies have been directly involved in the research. Hoping that we shall not offend anyone through omission, we wish to single out several executives who have been major sources of help and inspiration to us: Mike English, John Falzon, Tom Gillett, Donald Hughes, Linda Kanner, Dawn Lesh, Mary LoSardo, Claudia Marshall, David Richardson, and Fred Thiemann. We also wish to thank Allen Paison and Jeffrey Marr from Walker Research in Indianapolis who provided significant logistical assistance to us in managing our massive data collection effort for phase III.

Last but not least, we thank Bob Wallace, senior editor at The Free Press, who believed in this book project from the outset, and Glenda Bessler, an incredibly good secretary and friend to the Texas members of the team. Glenda spent many late hours hovering over her computer typing and retyping our chapter drafts. She did a wonderful job, as did

Michael Guiry, a graduate student, and Bridget Clayton, a secretary, at Duke University. Michael and Bridget contributed significantly to the completion of the chapters prepared in North Carolina. Their diligence, attention to detail, and responsiveness were excellent examples of service quality in action.

As for the three of us, we take great pleasure in bringing to you the product of our collaboration. We three have been intellectual partners and friends for many years and it is personally satisfying to us to publish this work. We shared equally in the book's preparation.

Valarie Zeithaml
A. Parasuraman
Leonard L. Berry

1

◇ ◇ ◇

SERVICE LEADERSHIP SPELLS PROFITS

Sᴇʀᴠɪᴄᴇ ǫᴜᴀʟɪᴛʏ is a central issue in America today. In a recent Gallup survey, executives ranked the improvement of service and tangible product quality as the single most critical challenge facing U.S. business.

One reason service quality has become such an important issue is that America's economy has become a service economy. Services account for approximately three-fourths of the gross national product and nine out of ten new jobs the economy creates. As David Birch writes:

> It used to be that we were good at growing things. We still are, but with virtually no people involved. Agricultural employment has gone from well over half of all jobs to about 2% of them.
>
> It used to be that we were good at making things. We still are, but with very few people involved. . . . Today, only 9% of American workers actually labor in factories.
>
> Yet, we have created millions of jobs. . . . It's not surprising that what these people are doing instead of making things is providing services.[1]

Virtually all organizations compete to some degree on the basis of service. It is difficult to name even one industry for which service matters are unimportant. Study the strategies of manufacturing companies such as Ford Motor Company or Corning Glass Works and what you find is a paramount role for service. Indeed, as the decade of the 1990's unfolds, more and more executives in manufacturing firms will be as keenly interested in *service quality* as executives in banking, health-care, and transportation businesses are today. As manufacturing executives find it increasingly difficult to establish sustainable, technology-based competitive advantages, they will direct added attention and resources to value-

1

added service as a truer source of superiority. And as manufacturers compete more on service, there will be less distinction between manufacturing and service businesses.

Services are also crucial to America's future as a worldwide competitor. The U.S. government is counting on significant growth in net service exports in the 1990's to play a key role in addressing the country's balance of trade problems. And yet, America's net positive trade balance in services fell steadily throughout the 1980's, prompting some observers to suggest that the United States is on the verge of taking the same international beating in services that it has already endured in manufacturing. The principal culprit is seen as mediocre service quality. As Quinn and Gagnon write:

> It will take hard and dedicated work not to dissipate our broad-based lead in services, as we did in manufacturing. Many of the same causes of lost position are beginning to appear. Daily we encounter the same inattention to quality, emphasis on scale economies rather than customers' concerns, and short-term financial orientation that earlier injured manufacturing.[2]

The central role for services in the American economy is a key factor behind service quality's rising prominence as an institutional and societal issue. Services are so much a part of what we produce, consume, and export in this nation that it would be surprising if we weren't concerned about quality.

A second factor behind service quality's rising prominence is that superior quality is proving to be a winning competitive strategy. McDonald's. Federal Express. Nordstrom. American Airlines. American Express. L. L. Bean. Domino's Pizza. Disney World. Club Med. Deluxe Corporation. Marriott. IBM. In every nook and cranny of the service economy, the leading companies are obsessed with service excellence. They use service to be different; they use service to increase productivity; they use service to earn the customers' loyalty; they use service to fan positive word-of-mouth advertising; they use service to seek some shelter from price competition.

Service excellence pays off richly for reasons we develop in more detail later in this chapter. With service excellence, everyone wins. Customers win. Employees win. Management wins. Stockholders win. Communities win. The country wins.

THE URGENT NEED FOR SERVICE LEADERSHIP

How do we explain the incongruity that service excellence pays off and yet is in such short supply? The signs of indifferent, careless, and incompetent service in America are everywhere.

In a national banking study, three out of ten consumers recall a service problem at their current or former financial institution, typically an error of one kind or another. More than half of those recalling problems deemed them serious enough to switch financial institutions or to close accounts.[3]

In an *Atlanta Journal* and *Atlanta Constitution* survey of readers, 91 percent of the respondents said that quality of service had declined over the previous 20 years. Wrote one reader: "The animals are running the zoo."[4]

Time magazine recently devoted a cover story to the service problem, claiming that "Personal service has become a maddeningly rare commodity in the American marketplace."[5]

The *Wall Street Journal*, in a story about health-care service, stated: "The problems are manifold: Bad diagnoses. Unnecessary surgery. Over prescribing or misrepresenting drugs. High rates of hospital infection. Lab-test errors. Faulty medical devices. Alcoholic or drug-addicted doctors."[6] Lowell Levin of Yale University's medical school advises surgery patients to use a magic marker to indicate just where on their bodies the surgery is to be done, claiming his advice wouldn't sound ridiculous if people only knew how often mistakes do occur.[7]

Stanley Marcus, retired chairman of Neiman-Marcus, admonishes specialty and department store retailers for forgetting their sales-service heritage. Marcus writes:

> Poor selling saved me $48,373 in 1983. That year, I decided I would not buy anything I didn't need unless someone sold it to me. Whenever I found something I wanted, but didn't encounter sales persuasiveness, I did not buy. By the end of the year, my savings total was $48,373.[8]

MANAGING IS NOT ENOUGH

The research that we present in this book documents the central role that leadership plays in delivering excellent service. We have seen firsthand how strong management commitment to service quality energizes and stimulates an organization to improved service performance. We have seen firsthand how role ambiguity, poor teamwork, and other neg-atives fester in a rudderless, leaderless environment, sapping an organi-zation's service quality.

True service leadership builds a climate for excellence that prevails over operational complexities, external market pressures, or any other impediments to quality service that might exist. Mediocre service in America is common, but it is not a given. In every single industry we have examples of companies delivering superb service. Excellent service is not a pipe dream; it is possible to overcome the conditions that foster service mediocrity. *The key is genuine service leadership at all levels of an organization—leadership that offers the direction and inspiration to sustain com-mitted servers.*

Managing is not enough. Service work can be difficult and demoralizing. Customers can be rude. Company policies can be suffocating. Sheer num-bers of customers to serve can be overwhelming. End-of-the-day fatigue can be desensitizing. Over time many service employees get "beat up" by the service role and become less effective with customers even as they gain technical experience that should produce the opposite result.

Listen to psychologist James Carr as he describes how a novel he read about the circus made him recognize the transformation he himself un-derwent in service roles:

> It was not the story line . . . that left its mark on me. It was the description of the social atmosphere through which the characters moved. All who lived under the big top—the freaks, the acrobats, even the animals—were real to each other. Everyone else—specifically anyone in the audience—was a "flatty."
>
> . . . I recalled how I had despaired, during a brief stint as a ticket agent during World War II, over the futility of trying to give individual attention to the masses of rail travelers clamoring to get somewhere . . . and I remembered the irritation I had felt when the crowds became unmanageable at several counter jobs I had held in my youth. There had been times when it seemed the only salvation was to retreat from involvement with individuals and to devote my attention exclusively to the specifics of the job at hand. When I did this, the customers became two-dimensional nonentities without personality or feelings. . . . At the time I had not referred to them as flatties but oh how descriptive was the term when I encountered it. . . . Even though I had treated people that way—often consider-ing it businesslike—I realized that I had always resented being treated as a flatty![9]

Few of us, like Carr, wish to be treated as a flatty by service providers. Few service providers, again like Carr, begin a new job treating customers in this way. Robotlike service traits almost always develop on the job.

People in service work need a vision in which they can believe, an achievement culture that challenges them to be the best they can be, a sense of team that nurtures and supports them, and role models that show them the way. This is the stuff of leadership.

In their book, *Leaders: The Strategies for Taking Charge*, Bennis and Nanus point out that the principal distinction between leaders and managers is that leaders emphasize the emotional and spiritual resources of an organization, its values, and aspirations, whereas managers emphasize the physical resources of the organization, such as raw materials, technology, and capital.[10]

The root cause of our quality malaise in America today—the reason service isn't better than it is despite the fruits of excellent service—is the insufficiency of service leadership. Too many service workers are overmanaged and underled. Thick policy manuals rule management's belief in good judgment of frontline servers. Memoranda from above supersede face-to-face, give-and-take dialogue with employees. The goal of profit takes precedence over the goal of providing a service good enough that people will pay a profit to have it.[11]

To materially improve service, we must devote more energy and attention in our businesses and business schools to the development of leadership values and capabilities. Otherwise, the temptation of service mediocrity will continue to win out over the promise of service excellence.

CHARACTERISTICS OF SERVICE LEADERS

Service leaders come in all shapes and sizes. They do not come from some kind of magical service cookie cutter. Having said this, there are some characteristics of service leadership about which it is useful to generalize. Here are some of the most important characteristics:

1. *Service vision.* Service leaders see service quality as a success key. They see service as integral to the organization's future, not as a peripheral issue. They believe fundamentally that superior service is a winning strategy, a profit strategy.

Regardless of the markets targeted, the menu of services offered, or the pricing policies followed, service leaders see quality of service as the foundation for competing. Whatever the specifics of the vision, the idea of service excellence is a central part.

Service leaders never waver in their commitment to service quality. They see service excellence as a never-ending journey in which the only effective option is to plug away toward better quality every day of every week of every month of every year. They understand that service quality is not a program; that there are no quick fixes, no magic formulas, no quality pills to swallow.

Service leaders understand that service excellence requires a full-court press—all of the time.* They understand that a company cannot turn the service issue on and off like a water faucet. As L. L. Bean, Inc., President Leon Gorman states: "A lot of people have fancy things to say about customer service, including me. But it's just a day-in, day-out, ongoing, never-ending, unremitting, persevering . . . type of activity."[12]

2. *High standards.* True service leaders aspire to legendary service; they realize that good service may not be good enough to differentiate their organization from other organizations.

Service leaders are interested in the details and nuances of service, seeing opportunities in small actions that competitors might consider trivial. They believe that how an organization handles the little things sets the tone for how it handles the big things. They also believe that the little things add up for the customer and make a difference. This is why Jim Daniel, CEO of the Friendly Bank in Oklahoma City has the bank's lobby floor polished daily. And why Robert Onstead, CEO of Randall's Food and Drugs in Houston, insists on lighting his parking lots so brightly that "customers could read newspapers in the parking lots at midnight if they wished to do so."[13]

Service leaders are zealous about doing the service right the first time. They value the goal of zero defects, striving continually to improve the reliability of service. They recognize the flip side of a 98 percent reliability rate, which is 2 percent unreliability. This is why Will Potter, CEO of Maryland-based Preston Trucking Company, has each employee agree in writing to abide by the company's service philosophy which states, in part:

> Once I make a commitment to a customer or another associate, I promise to fulfill it on time. I will do what I say when I say I will do it. . . . I understand that one claim or one mistake is one error too many. I promise to do my job right the first time and to continually seek performance improvement.

* For readers who are not basketball fans, we are using the phrase "full-court press" to mean unremitting vigilance.

3. In-the-field leadership style. Service leaders lead in the field, where the action is, rather than from their desks. They are visible to their people, endlessly coaching, praising, correcting, cajoling, sermonizing, observing, questioning, and listening. They emphasize two-way, personal communications because they know this is the best way to give shape, substance, and credibility to the service vision and the best way to learn what is really going on in the field.

Service leaders also employ their hands-on approach to build a climate of teamwork within the organization. They challenge the organizational unit to be excellent in service, not just the individual employee, using the influence of their offices to bring the team together frequently for meetings, rallies, and celebrations.

Sam Walton, the founder and chairman of retailing giant Wal-Mart Stores, Inc., practices in-the-field leadership as well as any senior executive in America today. Walton and other top Wal-Mart executives spend most of their time each week visiting stores, spreading the gospel, and listening to the sounds of the business. Each Friday the Wal-Mart management team reassembles in the Bentonville, Arkansas, headquarters for mandatory meetings in which they share insights from the field. On the next day several hundred headquarters personnel and managers visiting from the field come together in Wal-Mart's famous Saturday morning meeting, a potpourri of results reporting, plans presentations, cheers, hoopla, homespun philosophy, recognition of outstanding performers, bantering, and exhortations for improvement personally led by Sam Walton himself. With its own communications satellite, Wal-Mart has the capability to broadcast the Saturday meeting directly to its stores. As securities analyst Joseph Ellis once remarked in a speech: "Wal-Mart operates like a small company in terms of how it communicates with its people."[14]

4. Integrity. One of the essential characteristics of service leaders is personal integrity. The best leaders value doing the right thing—even when inconvenient or costly. They place a premium on being fair, consistent, and truthful—and, as a result, earn the trust of associates. As Peter Drucker writes: "The final requirement of effective leadership is to earn trust. Otherwise there won't be any followers—and the only definition of a leader is someone who has followers."[15]

Service leaders recognize the impossibility of building a service-minded attitude in an organization whose management lacks integrity. They recognize the interconnection between service excellence and employees' pride and understand that employees' pride is shaped in part by their perceptions of management fairness.

When executives buy and sell companies as though they were cattle, demonstrating scant interest in what happens to employees and customers as a result; when they inflate prices and then quickly mark the prices down so they can use the term *sale*, when they train and script salespeople to use bait-and-switch, scare, and other unethical tactics to pressure customers to buy what they don't need—these executives completely undermine their own credibility on the subject of service quality. Employees see for themselves that management cares not at all about servicing and satisfying customers. And most employees eventually ask themselves: "Why give my all to a company that lacks integrity? Why bust my chops for a company in which I do not believe?"[16]

Quality and integrity are inseparable, a point powerfully made in an essay entitled "The Quest for Quality":

> As the phrase "the honest workman" suggests, workmanship is founded in personal integrity. Those imbued with it have nothing but scorn for sloppiness, shabbiness, cheapness, sharp dealing or false fronts. Thus if the instinct of workmanship could be stimulated throughout the population, it would affect far more than the economy. In a "quality society," honesty, excellence, and the principle of giving full value for what we receive would become the rule of conduct both in business and personal relationships. What began as an effort to improve quality could end in a revolutionary improvement in the overall quality of life.[17]

THE PAYOFF OF QUALITY

Service leaders, as we have just noted, fundamentally believe that high quality pays off on the bottom line. Many executives, however, are not so sure. Many executives are not yet convinced that hard-dollar investments to improve service will come back as profit gains.

And these executives may be right. Investments to improve service may not come back as profit gains. Indeed, a lot of money is wasted in organizations every year in the name of quality improvement. From adding costly service features that are unimportant to customers to spending training money unwisely, it is quite common for organizations to throw money away pursuing better service quality. As a car-rental agent confesses: "The computer training was real good. I know how to do all this technical stuff, but nobody prepared me for dealing with all these different types of people."[18]

Actually improving service in the eyes of customers is what pays off. When service improvement investments lead to *perceived* service improvement, quality becomes a profit strategy.

The positive relationship between perceived quality and profitability is documented empirically. The massive data base from the Profit Impact of Market Strategy (PIMS) program shows this relationship unequivocally. In *The PIMS Principles*, Buzzell and Gale make the point about as clearly as it can be made:

> In the long run, the most important single factor affecting a business unit's performance is the quality of its products and services, relative to those of competitors. A quality edge boosts performance in two ways:
>
> - In the short run, superior quality yields increased profits via premium prices. As Frank Perdue, the well-known chicken grower, put it: "Customers will go out of their way to buy a superior product, and you can charge them a toll for the trip." Consistent with Perdue's theory, PIMS businesses that ranked in the top third on relative quality sold their products or services, on average, at prices 5–6% higher (relative to competition) than those in the bottom third.
> - In the longer term, superior and/or improving relative quality is the more effective way for a business to grow. Quality leads to both market expansion and gains in market share. The resulting growth in volume means that a superior-quality competitor gains scale advantages over rivals. As a result, even when there are short-run costs connected with improving quality, over a period of time these costs are usually offset by scale economies. Evidence of this is the fact that, on average, businesses with superior quality products have costs about equal to those of their leading competitors. As long as their selling prices are not out of line, they continue to grow while still earning superior profit margins.[19]

Exhibit 1–1, from the PIMS data base, graphically shows the positive relationship between relative perceived quality and return on sales or return on investment.

QUALITY CREATES TRUE CUSTOMERS

Excellent service pays off because it creates true customers—customers who are glad they selected a firm after the service experience, customers who will use the firm again and sing the firm's praises to others.

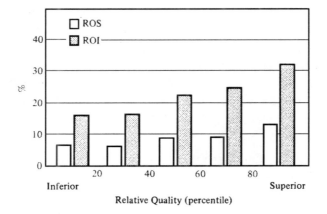

Exhibit 1-1 The Quality/Profit Relationship
SOURCE: Robert D. Buzzell and Bradley T. Gale, *The PIMS Principles* (New York: Free Press, 1987), p. 107.

True customers are like annuities—they keep pumping revenue into the firm's coffers. Stew Leonard, the much-heralded retailer whose Norwalk, Connecticut, food store annually does $3,000 in business per square foot, understands the annuity analogy as well as anyone:

> We should never let a customer leave the store unhappy because we look at each customer as a potential $50,000 asset. An average customer spends $100 a week on food shopping. That's more than $5,000 a year, and more than $50,000 over ten years. Customer service is big business when you look at the long-term picture.[20]

The essence of services marketing is service. Whereas the marketing textbooks stress the four Ps of marketing—product, place, promotion, and price—in a service business the most important competitive weapon is the fifth P of *performance*. It is the performance of the service that separates one service firm from others; it is the performance of the service that creates true customers who buy more, are more loyal, pay Frank Perdue's "toll for the trip," and who spread favorable word of mouth.

Excellent service differentiates otherwise similar competitors in a way that is important to customers. Whereas competing service firms often look the same with similar facilities, equipment, and menus of services, these firms do not feel the same to customers. A genuinely warm greeting from a service provider or the graceful handling of a special request can help one firm seem very different to its customers than other suppliers of similar services.

Thus, it is critical to make the distinction between services and service. *Competitors commonly offer the same services and different service.* That is why James Robinson, CEO of American Express Company, says: "Quality is our only form of patent protection."[21]

In effect, excellent service companies perform better on the bottom line because they perform better for their customers. Customers respond to these firms because they perceive more value in their offers than in competitive offerings. Value is the customer's "overall assessment of the utility of a product based on perceptions of what is received and what is given."[22] The concept of value helps explain how companies with strong service reputations are often able to charge higher prices than their competitors. Customers have to expend more than money to use a service; they also have to bear nonmonetary prices, for example, time and psychic cost.[23] These customers may be quite willing to assume more monetary cost to reduce nonmonetary cost and/or to obtain an otherwise stronger service.

QUALITY LEADS TO EFFICIENCIES

The PIMS data base shows that companies with high relative perceived quality have a cost of doing business that is similar to their main competitors. This is so even though quality improvement frequently involves increased investment in technology, marketing research, employee training, performance measurement, reward systems, and so forth.

What drives down costs most significantly is market share growth. Companies with high market shares benefit costwise from scale economies. Companies with high market shares built through high quality benefit from these scale economies *and from higher revenues due to heavy sales volume and premium prices.*

Quality improvement also leads to operational efficiencies beyond those associated with scale economies. The reality is that service errors and foul-ups add cost to the service delivery system. From computer time to fix account errors to more telephone lines to handle customer problems, service sloppiness steals from the bottom line.

In the early 1980s, a Merrill Lynch & Company, Inc. task force concluded that the firm's direct cost of service snafus was $210 million a year. This included the costs involved in staffing departments dedicated to correcting problems and errors.[24] Audits by Technical Assistance Research Programs, Inc. (TARP) at over a dozen financial service firms show that poor service and ineffective customer communications cause up to one-third of the total workload.[25]

Raymond Larkin, executive vice-president of operations at American Express, makes the point:

> I can't emphasize enough that quality is as bottom line as a company can get. This is as true in a service business as it is in manufacturing. For example, in our Card business, there is rework if errors are made in the first place—if remittances are not processed, if billings are incorrect, if establishments are not paid on time, if Cardmember benefits are not properly communicated. All this generates inquiries and additional processing—or what we call "avoidable input." Reducing avoidable input is the service equivalent to reducing rejects in manufacturing.[26]

The potential payoff from service excellence is considerable. Quality does pay. We know this from the PIMS research. We know this from the TARP research. We know this from the many companies we have worked with and observed closely over the years. And we know it from our own empirical research in service quality that we have written this book to share.

OVERVIEW OF THE BOOK

This book integrates the concepts, ideas, and findings that have emerged from an ongoing, multiphase study of service quality which we started in 1983. From this research, sponsored by the Marketing Science Institute in Cambridge, Massachusetts, we have developed a conceptual model of service quality and a methodology for measuring customer perceptions of service quality. We also have developed many ideas about what companies need to do to improve service quality.

We use our model as a framework for the book as it provides a structure for understanding service quality, measuring it, diagnosing service-quality problems, and deriving solutions to the problems—the very subjects an executive wishing to improve quality needs to entertain. We refer to the model as the *gaps model* because it features discrepancies or gaps that need to be closed to offer excellent service.

In chapter 2 we develop the customer part of our model, defining the concept and dimensions of service quality. In chapter 3 we present the managerial part of the model, focusing on four gaps that cause service-quality problems. In chapters 4 through 7 we take a closer look at these four gaps; in each chapter we focus on the underlying reasons for a gap and make suggestions for closing it. In chapter 8 we offer suggestions on how to get started in a service-improvement effort, a challenge that often appears to be overwhelming. And in chapter 9, the final chapter, we discuss emerging service quality issues and challenges for the decade of the 1990's. The book's appendixes include descriptions of our research methods and our survey instruments.

2

◇ ◇ ◇

THE CUSTOMERS' VIEW
OF SERVICE QUALITY

WHEN WE STARTED our research program in service quality, we expected to find a varied and rich literature that would guide us. We found nothing of the kind! Instead we found a literature almost exclusively devoted to tangible goods quality, defined in terms of conformance to manufacturers' specifications.[1] As a result, quality control principles and practices that we uncovered, while pertinent to evaluating and ensuring goods quality, were inadequate for understanding service quality. This inadequacy stems from the three fundamental ways services differ from goods in terms of how they are produced, consumed, and evaluated.

First, services are basically *intangible*. Because they are performances and experiences rather than objects, precise manufacturing specifications concerning uniform quality can rarely be set. Unlike automobiles and audiocassettes, airline transportation and aerobic exercises cannot be measured, tested, and verified in advance of sale to assure quality. Moreover, when what is being sold is purely a performance, the criteria customers use to evaluate it may be complex and difficult to capture precisely.

Second, services—especially those with a high labor content—are *heterogeneous*: their performance often varies from producer to producer, from customer to customer, and from day to day. The quality of the interactions that bank tellers, flight attendants, and insurance agents have with customers can rarely be standardized to ensure uniformity the way quality of goods produced in a manufacturing plant can.

Third, production and consumption of many services are *inseparable*. Quality in services often occurs during service delivery, usually in an interaction between the customer and the provider, rather than being engineered at the manufacturing plant and delivered intact to the customer. Unlike goods producers, service providers do not have the benefit

15

of a factory serving as a buffer between production and consumption. Service customers are often in the service factory, observing and evaluating the production process as they experience the service.

While the literature on quality has been predominantly goods-oriented, a few contributions have focused on service quality.[2] From these writings emerge the following themes:

- Service quality is more difficult for customers to evaluate than goods quality. Therefore, the criteria customers use to evaluate service quality may be more difficult for the marketer to comprehend. How customers evaluate investment services offered by a stockbroker is more complicated and varied than how they evaluate insulation materials. Customers' assessment of the quality of health-care services is more complex and difficult than their assessment of the quality of automobiles.
- Customers do not evaluate service quality solely on the outcome of a service (e.g., how a customer's hair looks after a hair cut); they also consider the process of service delivery (e.g., how involved, responsive, and friendly the hair stylist is during the hair cut).
- The only criteria that count in evaluating service quality are defined by customers. Only customers judge quality; all other judgments are essentially irrelevant. Specifically, service-quality perceptions stem from how well a provider performs vis-à-vis customers' expectations about how the provider should perform.

EXPLORATORY CUSTOMER STUDY

The sparse literature on service quality provided us with several general insights. Clearly, it was not rich enough to develop a comprehensive conceptual foundation for understanding and improving service quality. A number of key questions remained unanswered: How exactly do customers evaluate the quality of a service? Do they directly make a global evaluation or do they assess specific facets of a service in arriving at an overall evaluation? If the latter, what are the multiple facets or dimensions on which they evaluate the service? Do those dimensions vary across services and different customer segments? If customers' expectations play a crucial role in the assessment of service quality, which factors shape and influence those expectations?

To seek answers to these and related questions we undertook an exploratory study consisting of 12 customer focus-group interviews, 3 in each of four service sectors: retail banking, credit cards, securities brokerage, and product repair and maintenance. These service businesses vary along key attributes used to categorize services.[3] For example, retail banking and credit-card services provide immediate customer benefits, while securities-brokerage and product-repair services provide more enduring benefits. Although product repair and maintenance services concern customers' tangible possessions, the other three services pertain to customers' intangible (financial) assets. Banking and securities-brokerage services are more labor intensive and interactive than the other two.

We purposely selected a broad spectrum of consumer services to study in this first phase of our research because we were looking for service-quality insights that would transcend the boundaries of specific industries. We also varied the composition of the focus groups to ensure that our findings would be generalizable to a variety of settings. Additional details concerning the composition and conduct of the focus groups are outlined in "Focus-Group Interviews."

FOCUS-GROUP INTERVIEWS

We controlled the composition of the 12 focus groups (3 groups per service sector) in accordance with guidelines traditionally followed in the marketing research field. Specifically, we screened respondents to ensure that they had engaged in one or more transactions pertaining to the service in question within the previous three months. Thus each focus group consisted of recent users of one of the four services. Between 8 and 12 respondents participated in each focus group. To maintain similarity among members and assure maximum participation, we assigned respondents to groups on the basis of sex and age. Six of the 12 groups included only males and 6 included only females. However, we interviewed at least one male group and one female group for each of the four services. Respondents in each group were roughly in the same age bracket; but the three focus groups for each service category covered different age brackets to ascertain the viewpoints of a broad cross section of customers.

We conducted eight focus groups in a metropolitan area in southwestern United States. We distributed the remaining four groups—one on the West Coast, one in the Midwest, and two in the East—to achieve geographic diversity.

A nationally recognized company from each of the four service sectors sponsored and participated in our study. We did not, however, reveal the identities of these firms to the focus-group participants because our interest was in customers' quality evaluations in a service category in general, as opposed to their assessment of the participating firm in that category.

One member of the research team served as the moderator for each of the focus groups. The questions we asked to stimulate discussion covered topics such as instances of, and reasons for, satisfaction and dissatisfaction with the service; descriptions of an ideal service (e.g., ideal bank or ideal credit card); the meaning of service quality; factors important in evaluating service quality; and performance expectations concerning the service.

FOCUS-GROUP FINDINGS

Through the focus-group interviews we learned a great deal about how customers view service quality. Customers talked about many things—their expectations, their priorities, their experiences. They told us about high quality and low quality. They talked about many different attributes, some dealing with the service itself; others dealing with the person delivering the service.

Even though the specific examples and experiences the respondents shared with us were unique to the service category being discussed, we detected a number of underlying patterns in the responses—patterns remarkably consistent across all four sets of focus-group interviews. These common patterns offered us valuable insights about how customers define and evaluate service quality.

Definition of Service Quality. The focus groups unambiguously supported the notion that the key to ensuring good service quality is meeting or exceeding what customers expect from the service. One female participant described a situation when a repairman not only fixed her broken appliance but also explained what had gone wrong and how she could fix it herself if a similar problem occurred in the future. She rated the quality of this service excellent because it exceeded her expectations. A male respondent in a banking-services focus group described the frustration he felt when his bank would not cash his payroll check from a nationally known employer because it was postdated by one day. When someone else in the group pointed out legal constraints preventing the bank from cashing his check, he responded, "Well, nobody in the bank explained that to me!" Not receiving an explanation in the bank, this respondent perceived that the bank was unwilling, rather than unable, to cash the check. This in turn resulted in a perception of poor service quality.

Similar experiences, both positive and negative, were described by customers in every focus group. It was clear to us that judgments of high and low service quality depend on how customers perceive the actual service performance in the context of what they expected. Therefore service quality, as perceived by customers, can be defined as *the extent of discrepancy between customers' expectations or desires and their perceptions.*

Factors Influencing Expectations. The common themes emerging from the focus groups suggested several key factors that might shape customers' expectations. First, what customers hear from other customers—*word-of-mouth communications*—is a potential determinant of expectations. For instance, several respondents in our product-repair focus groups indicated that the high quality of service they expected from the repair firms they chose stemmed from the recommendations of their friends and neighbors.

Second, in each of the four sets of focus groups, respondents' expectations appeared to vary somewhat depending on their individual characteristics and circumstances, suggesting thereby that *personal needs* of customers might moderate their expectations to a certain degree. For example, in the credit-card focus groups, while some customers expected credit-card companies to provide them with the maximum possible credit limits, other customers wished that their credit-card companies were more stringent than they then were.

Third, the extent of *past experience* with using a service could also influence customers' expectation levels. More experienced participants in the securities-brokerage focus groups, for instance, seemed to have somewhat lower expectations regarding brokers' behavioral attributes such as friendliness and politeness; however, they appeared to be more demanding with respect to brokers' technical competence and effectiveness.

Fourth, *external communications* from service providers play a key role in shaping customers' expectations. Under external communications we include a variety of direct and indirect messages conveyed by service firms to customers: a bank's print advertisement promising the friendliest tellers in town, a television commercial for a credit card touting its acceptability around the world, a repair firm's receptionist guaranteeing the arrival of a service representative at an appointed time, or a brokerage firm's glossy brochures implying a promise of superior service.

One factor whose influence on expectations is subsumed under the general influence of external communications is price. This factor plays an important role in shaping expectations, particularly those of prospective customers of a service. To illustrate, for customers contemplating the purchase of brokerage services for the first time, price is likely to influence their choice of a certain type of broker (e.g. a full-service versus a discount broker) as well as their expectations from the chosen broker. The securities-brokerage focus groups we conducted, while consisting of respondents who were already using brokerage services, did reveal differences in expectations between users of full-service and discount brokers, implying a link between price levels and expectation levels.

Dimensions of Service Quality. Perhaps the most revealing and most unique insights emerging from our focus groups concern the criteria used by customers in judging service quality. The numerous examples and experiences that respondents shared with us in the 12 focus groups provided us with a rich reservoir of customers' expectations as reflected by specific questions that customers apparently ask, and answer, in assessing service quality. After we sifted through these questions several times, it was clear that the same general criteria underlay sets of service-specific questions spanning the four sectors. We identified ten general criteria or dimensions and labeled them tangibles, reliability, responsiveness, competence, courtesy, credibility, security, access, communication, and understanding the customer. Exhibit 2–1 contains concise definitions of these dimensions and illustrates each dimension with service-specific evaluative questions emerging from the focus groups.

The ten dimensions defined and illustrated in exhibit 2–1 are not necessarily independent of one another. For instance, facets of credibility and security may indeed overlap somewhat. Because our focus-group research was exploratory and qualitative, measurement of possible overlap across the ten dimensions had to await a subsequent quantitative phase of research (described in the next section). We are confident that the set of ten general dimensions of service quality is exhaustive and appropriate for assessing quality in a broad variety of services. Even though the *specific* evaluative criteria may vary from service to service, the general dimensions underlying those criteria are captured by our set of ten.

In summary, from our exploratory study we were able to (1) define service quality as the discrepancy between customers' expectations and perceptions; (2) suggest key factors—word-of-mouth communications, personal needs, past experience, and external communications—that influence customers' expectations; and (3) identify ten general dimensions that represent the evaluative criteria customers use to assess service quality. Exhibit 2–2 provides a pictorial summary of these findings.

Dimension and Definition	Examples of Specific Questions Raised by Customers
Tangibles: Appearance of physical facilities, equipment, personnel, and communication materials.	· Are the bank's facilities attractive? · Is my stockbroker dressed appropriately? · Is my credit card statement easy to understand? · Do the tools used by the repair person look modern?
Reliability: Ability to perform the promised service dependably and accurately.	· When a loan officer says she will call me back in 15 minutes, does she do so? · Does the stockbroker follow my exact instructions to buy or sell? · Is my credit card statement free of errors? · Is my washing machine repaired right the first time?
Responsiveness: Willingness to help customers and provide prompt service.	· When there is a problem with my bank statement, does the bank resolve the problem quickly? · Is my stockbroker willing to answer my questions? · Are charges for returned merchandise credited to my account promptly? · Is the repair firm willing to give me a specific time when the repair person will show up?
Competence: Possession of the required skills and knowledge to perform the service.	· Is the bank teller able to process my transactions without fumbling around? · Does my brokerage firm have the research capabilities to accurately track market developments? · When I call my credit card company, is the person at the other end able to answer my questions? · Does the repair person appear to know what he is doing?
Courtesy: Politeness, respect, consideration, and friendliness of contact personnel.	· Does the bank teller have a pleasant demeanor? · Does my broker refrain from acting busy or being rude when I ask questions? · Are the telephone operators in the credit card company consistently polite when answering my calls? · Does the repair person take off his muddy shoes before stepping on my carpet?

(continued)

Exhibit 2–1 Ten Dimensions of Service Quality

Dimension and Definition	Examples of Specific Questions Raised by Customers
Credibility: Trustworthiness, believability, honesty of the service provider.	• Does the bank have a good reputation? • Does my broker refrain from pressuring me to buy? • Are the interest rates/fees charged by my credit card company consistent with the services provided? • Does the repair firm guarantee its services?
Security: Freedom from danger, risk, or doubt.	• Is it safe for me to use the bank's automatic teller machines? • Does my brokerage firm know where my stock certificate is? • Is my credit card safe from unauthorized use? • Can I be confident that the repair job was done properly?
Access: Approachability and ease of contact.	• How easy is it for me to talk to senior bank officials when I have a problem? • Is it easy to get through to my broker over the telephone? • Does the credit card company have a 24-hour, toll-free telephone number? • Is the repair service facility conveniently located?
Communication: Keeping customers informed in language they can understand and listening to them.	• Can the loan officer explain clearly the various charges related to the mortgage loan? • Does my broker avoid using technical jargon? • When I call my credit card company, are they willing to listen to me? • Does the repair firm call when they are unable to keep a scheduled repair appointment?
Understanding the Customer: Making the effort to know customers and their needs.	• Does someone in my bank recognize me as a regular customer? • Does my broker try to determine what my specific financial objectives are? • Is the credit limit set by my credit card company consistent with what I can afford (i.e., neither too high nor too low)? • Is the repair firm willing to be flexible enough to accommodate *my* schedule?

Exhibit 2-1 Continued

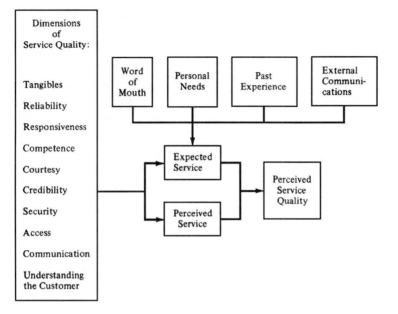

Exhibit 2-2 Customer Assessment of Service Quality

SERVQUAL: AN INSTRUMENT
FOR MEASURING SERVICE QUALITY

Building on the conceptual definition of service quality and the ten evaluative dimensions from our exploratory research, we embarked on a quantitative research phase to develop an instrument for measuring customers' perceptions of service quality. To ensure that our instrument would have sound statistical properties and broad acceptability, this phase of our research involved customer surveys in five different service sectors: product repair and maintenance, retail banking, long-distance telephone, securities brokerage, and credit cards. Details of these surveys are summarized in "Development of SERVQUAL."

Our quantitative research phase resulted in a parsimonious instrument (SERVQUAL) consisting of two sections: (1) An expectations section containing 22 statements to ascertain the general expectations of customers concerning a service, and (2) a perceptions section containing a matching set of 22 statements to measure customers' assessments of a specific firm within the service category. The instructions and statements for the two sections of SERVQUAL are presented in appendix A.[4]

DEVELOPMENT OF SERVQUAL

In developing SERVQUAL—our instrument for measuring customers' perceptions of service quality—we followed well-established procedures for designing scales to measure constructs that are not directly observable. We developed 97 items capturing the 10 dimensions of service quality identified in our exploratory phase. We then recast each item into a pair of statements—one to measure expectations about firms in general within the service category being investigated, and the other to measure perceptions about the particular firm whose service quality was being assessed.

Sample expectation statement: "When these firms promise to do something by a certain time, they should do so."

Sample perception statement: "When XYZ promises to do something by a certain time, it does so."

A seven-point scale ranging from 7 (strongly agree) to 1 (strongly disagree) accompanied each statement.

We refined and condensed the 97-item instrument through a series of repeated data-collection and -analysis steps. We performed this instrument purification to eliminate items that failed to discriminate well among respondents with differing quality perceptions about firms. We gathered data for the initial refinement of the 97-item instrument from a quota sample of 200 customers, divided equally between males and females. Included in the sample were recent users of one of the following five services: appliance repair and maintenance, retail banking, long-distance telephone, securities brokerage, and credit cards. We converted the raw questionnaire data into perception-minus-expectation scores for the various items. These difference scores could range from $+6$ to -6, with more positive scores representing higher perceived service quality. We analyzed the difference scores using several statistical analyses. These analyses resulted in the elimination of roughly two-thirds of the original items and the consolidation of several overlapping quality dimensions into new, combined dimensions. To verify the reliability and validity of the condensed scale, we administered it to four independent samples of approximately 190 customers each. We gathered data on the service quality of four nationally known firms: a bank, a credit-card issuer, an appliance repair-and-maintenance firm, and a long-distance telephone company. Analysis of data from the four samples led to additional refinement of the instrument and confirmed its reliability and validity. The final instrument consists of 22 items, spanning the five dimensions of service quality described in the chapter: tangibles, reliability, responsiveness, assurance, and empathy.

The various statistical analyses conducted in constructing SERVQUAL revealed considerable correlation among items representing several of the original ten dimensions. In particular, the correlations suggested consolidation of the last seven dimensions listed in exhibits 2–1 and 2–2 into two broader dimensions labeled *assurance* and *empathy*. The remaining dimensions—*tangibles*, *reliability*, and *responsiveness*—remained intact throughout the scale development and refinement process. Exhibit 2–3 shows the correspondence between the original ten dimensions and SERVQUAL's five dimensions.

When we examined the content of the final items making up the two new dimensions (assurance and empathy), we found that the items still

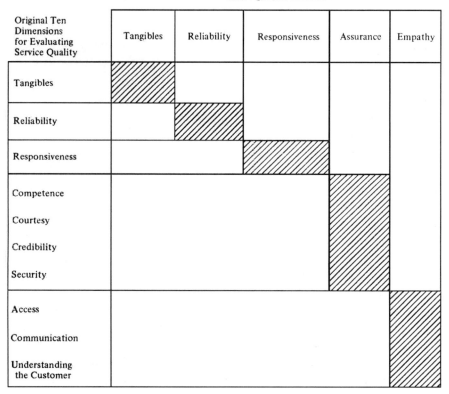

SERVQUAL Dimensions

Original Ten Dimensions for Evaluating Service Quality	Tangibles	Reliability	Responsiveness	Assurance	Empathy
Tangibles	▨				
Reliability		▨			
Responsiveness			▨		
Competence				▨	
Courtesy				▨	
Credibility				▨	
Security				▨	
Access					▨
Communication					▨
Understanding the Customer					▨

Exhibit 2–3 Correspondence between SERVQUAL Dimensions and Original Ten Dimensions for Evaluating Service Quality

represented key features of the seven dimensions that were consolidated. Therefore, although SERVQUAL had only five distinct dimensions, they captured facets of all of the ten originally conceptualized dimensions. The items making up the consolidated dimensions also suggested concise definitions for them. These definitions, along with the definitions of the three original dimensions that remained intact, follow:

Tangibles	Appearance of physical facilities, equipment, personnel, and communication materials
Reliability	Ability to perform the promised service dependably and accurately
Responsiveness:	Willingness to help customers and provide prompt service
Assurance:	Knowledge and courtesy of employees and their ability to convey trust and confidence
Empathy:	Caring, individualized attention the firm provides its customers

RELATIVE IMPORTANCE
OF THE SERVQUAL DIMENSIONS

The five SERVQUAL dimensions, by virtue of being derived from systematic analysis of customers' ratings from hundreds of interviews in several service sectors, are a concise representation of the core criteria that customers employ in evaluating service quality. As such, it is reasonable to speculate that customers would consider all five criteria to be quite important. In fact, when we asked users of credit-card, repair-and-maintenance, long-distance telephone, and retail banking services to rate the importance of each SERVQUAL dimension on a scale of 1 (not all important) to 10 (extremely important), we found that all five dimensions were considered critical. As exhibit 2–4 reveals, the mean importance ratings for reliability, responsiveness, assurance, and empathy are above 9 for all four services; the mean ratings for tangibles, while somewhat low by comparison, are still in the upper end of the 10-point scale, ranging from 7.14 to 8.56.

Anticipating that the mean importance ratings may not reveal a clear picture of the relative importance of the five dimensions, we also asked

Exhibit 2-4 Importance of SERVQUAL Dimensions in Four Service Sectors

	Mean Importance Rating on 10-Point Scale*	Percentage of Respondents Indicating Dimension Is Most Important
Credit-Card Customers (n = 187)		
Tangibles	7.43	0.6
Reliability	9.45	48.6
Responsiveness	9.37	19.8
Assurance	9.25	17.5
Empathy	9.09	13.6
Repair-and-Maintenance Customers (n = 183)		
Tangibles	8.48	1.2
Reliability	9.64	57.2
Responsiveness	9.54	19.9
Assurance	9.62	12.0
Empathy	9.30	9.6
Long-Distance Telephone Customers (n = 184)		
Tangibles	7.14	0.6
Reliability	9.67	60.6
Responsiveness	9.57	16.0
Assurance	9.29	12.6
Empathy	9.25	10.3
Bank Customers (n = 177)		
Tangibles	8.56	1.1
Reliability	9.44	42.1
Responsiveness	9.34	18.0
Assurance	9.18	13.6
Empathy	9.30	25.1

* Scale ranges from 1 (not at all important) to 10 (extremely important).

the respondents which one dimension they would choose as being the most critical in their assessment of service quality. The respondents' choices, summarized in exhibit 2-4, clearly show that reliability is the most critical dimension, *regardless of the service being studied.* The results contained in exhibit 2-4, when considered collectively, imply an important message from customers to service providers: Appear neat and organized, be responsive, be reassuring, be empathetic, and most of all, be reliable—*do what you say you are going to do.*

We have used the SERVQUAL instrument in many different studies since we initially developed and tested it. Results from those studies have consistently shown reliability to be the most important dimension, and tangibles the least important. Most recently, we asked samples averaging about four hundred customers of each of five nationally known companies (two banks, two insurance companies, and a long-distance telephone company) to allocate a total of 100 points across the five dimensions according to how important they perceived each dimension to be. Based on responses from 1,936 customers, the average allocations received by the five dimensions are as shown in exhibit 2–5. The patterns of point-allocations by customers of each of the five companies were essentially similar to the consolidated pie chart (exhibit 2–5). Even though it is possible that the relative rankings of the dimensions as perceived by customers might change in the future, we are confident that the number one concern of customers today, regardless of type of service, is reliability; and the facet that matters the least to current customers in assessing quality of service is tangibles (the importance of tangibles as a quality cue to *potential* customers may be higher, however).

PERFORMANCE ALONG THE SERVQUAL DIMENSIONS

As perceived by customers, how well are service companies doing along the SERVQUAL dimensions? Results from our five-company

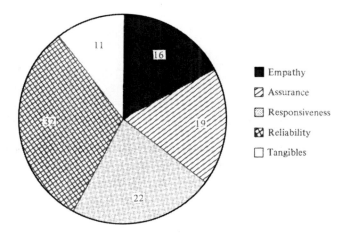

Exhibit 2–5 Relative Importance of SERVQUAL Dimensions when Customers Allocate 100 Points

study are very revealing. Exhibit 2–6 shows the mean SERVQUAL scores (i.e., perception-expectation scores) by dimension for the total customer sample. In this exhibit, the more negative the SERVQUAL score, the more serious the service-quality shortfall in the eyes of customers. Notice how the single most important dimension of service, reliability, has the most negative SERVQUAL score. And the second most important dimension, responsiveness, has the second most negative SERVQUAL score. The least important dimension, tangibles, has a slightly positive SERVQUAL score, implying that the companies in our study on average exceeded customers' expectations on this dimension! Clearly, there is a mismatch between the priorities expressed by customers and the levels of quality delivered by the companies.

Exhibit 2–7 shows the average SERVQUAL scores (aggregated across all five dimensions) for each company in our study. Two scores are shown for each company: an unweighted score, which is the simple average of the scores on the five dimensions, and a weighted score, which is an average that takes into account the relative weights assigned by customers when they allocated 100 points to the five dimensions. (Procedures for computing the unweighted and weighted scores, as well as other potential applications of the SERVQUAL scale and data, are given in appendix A.)

The negative SERVQUAL scores (both unweighted and weighted) across the board clearly show that there is room for service-quality im-

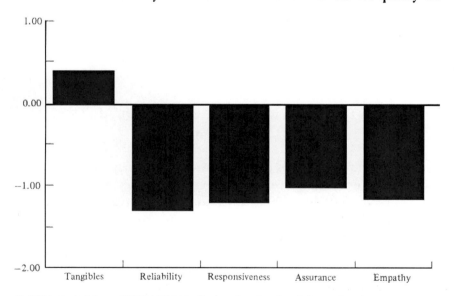

Exhibit 2–6 Mean SERVQUAL Scores by Service Dimension (n = 1,936)

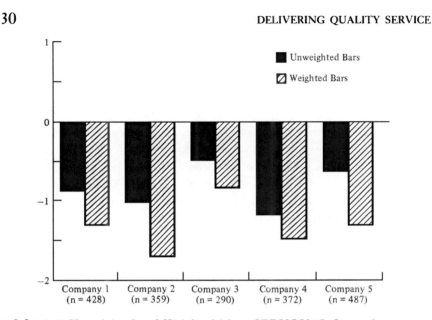

Exhibit 2–7 Unweighted and Weighted Mean SERVQUAL Scores by Company

provement in every company in our study. Even more significant is that the weighted scores are more negative than the unweighted scores in all five companies! This indicates that each company is performing most poorly on facets that are most critical to customers. The discrepancy between the unweighted and weighted scores in each company suggests the potential opportunity for improving quality of service perceptions by shifting emphasis and resources to the more critical facets of the service.

IMPACT OF SERVICE PROBLEMS ON QUALITY PERCEPTIONS

Are customers' perceptions of quality of service influenced by whether or not they experienced a recent service problem? Does satisfactory resolution of service problems improve service quality perceptions? We explored these questions in our five-company study. The results, summarized in exhibit 2–8, are revealing.

Exhibit 2–8 shows the average SERVQUAL scores (aggregated across all five dimensions and all five companies), broken out by the following pairs of customer subgroups: (1) customers who had experienced a recent service problem and those who had not; and (2) among customers who

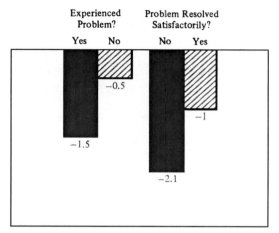

Exhibit 2–8 SERVQUAL Scores for Different Sample Groups

had experienced service problems, those who felt their problems were satisfactorily resolved and those who did not feel that way.[5] Clearly, when customers experience a service problem their perceptions of service quality are adversely affected. Moreover, companies fare best when they prevent service problems altogether and fare worst when service problems occur and are not resolved to the customers' satisfaction.

The implications of the findings summarized in exhibit 2–8 are clear: The most important thing a service company can do is *be reliable*—that is, perform the service dependably and accurately . . . do it right the first time. When a service problem does crop up, however, all is not lost . . . unless the company ignores it. In other words, by resolving the problem to the customer's satisfaction—by performing the service *very* right the second time—the company can significantly improve customer-retention rates.

At a time when many service companies view complaining customers with disdain—in the words of a focus-group participant in our exploratory research: "When you have a problem with their service they treat you like you have a disease!"—those companies that are truly dedicated to satisfactory problem resolution can reap handsome dividends. Research conducted by Technical Assistance Research Programs, Inc. (TARP), a consulting firm specializing in the study of customers' complaints, has shown that the average return from investments made to satisfactorily handle customers' complaints and inquiries ranges from 100 percent (for marketers of durable goods such as washing machines and refrigerators) to 170 percent (for banks).[6] Companies that epitomize exemplary quality of service are well aware of the excellent returns from resolving customers' problems to their satisfaction. Maryanne Rasmussen, vice-president of worldwide quality at one such company, American Express, nicely sums up the benefits of proper problem resolution: "The formula I use is: Better complaint handling equals higher customer satisfaction equals higher brand loyalty equals higher profitability."[7]

IMPACT OF QUALITY PERCEPTIONS ON WILLINGNESS TO RECOMMEND

Word-of-mouth recommendations (i.e., recommendations from friends and relatives) play a much greater role in customers' purchases of services than in their purchases of goods.[8] In light of the importance of word-of-mouth communications, we examined the association between customers' perceptions of the quality of service rendered by a company and their willingness to recommend the company to their friends. The results (aggregated across all five companies) are summarized in exhibit 2–9.

As the SERVQUAL scores represented by the bar chart in exhibit 2–9 show, there is a dramatic difference between the quality perceptions of customers who would and those who would not recommend their service companies to their friends. Clearly, a substantial improvement in customers' perceptions of a company's quality of service is required before they become positive spokespersons for it. Alternatively, striving to perform all facets of a service flawlessly the first time—and satisfactorily resolving any flaws that may occur—not only enhances a customer's

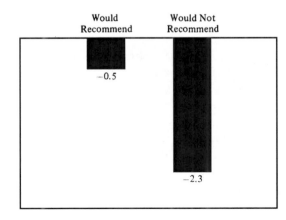

Exhibit 2–9 SERVQUAL Scores for Customers Who Would and Would Not Recommend the Company to a Friend

service-quality perceptions but also greatly increases his or her likelihood of recommending the company to prospective customers.

SUMMARY

In this chapter we reviewed a stream of customer research consisting of a series of qualitative studies (focus groups) followed by a series of quantitative studies (customer surveys). The qualitative phase of the research yielded a definition of service quality (i.e., discrepancy between customers' expectations and perceptions), identified the factors that influence customers' expectations (word of mouth, personal needs, past experience, and external communications from service providers), and revealed ten general dimensions or evaluative criteria that customers use in assessing service quality. A major outcome of the quantitative phase of our research was SERVQUAL—the 22-item instrument for measuring customers' expectations and perceptions along five quality dimensions (tangibles, reliability, responsiveness, assurance, and empathy). Studies conducted in the quantitative phase also illuminated the relative importance of the five dimensions (reliability most important; tangibles least important) and indicated how well service companies are performing along those dimensions. The collective findings from these studies suggest key opportunities for companies to improve their quality of service as perceived by customers. The findings also emphasize the significant benefits that companies can reap by providing superior service quality.

As revealed by our customer research described in this chapter, the key to delivering high-quality service is to balance customers' expectations and perceptions and close the gaps between the two. The SERVQUAL methodology can help determine where and how serious the gaps are. In attempting to close SERVQUAL gaps, a company would benefit from an understanding of internal (i.e., within-company) shortfalls or gaps that might be responsible for the external (i.e., customer-perceived) shortfalls. A major component of our multiphase study focused on identifying such internal gaps and relating them to customers' perceptions of service quality. The findings from this component of our study are the focus of the next chapter.

3

◇ ◇ ◇

POTENTIAL CAUSES OF SERVICE-QUALITY SHORTFALLS

EXECUTIVES STRIVING TO ACHIEVE a distinctive position and a sustainable advantage in today's increasingly competitive business world no doubt realize the importance of delivering superior quality service by meeting or exceeding customers' expectations. However, simply believing in the importance of providing excellent service quality is not enough. Executives who are truly dedicated to service quality must put in motion a continuous process for: (1) monitoring customers' perceptions of service quality; (2) identifying the causes of service-quality shortfalls; and (3) taking appropriate action to improve the quality of service.

The SERVQUAL approach discussed in the preceding chapter focused on assessing and understanding customers' perceptions of service quality. This chapter focuses on deficiencies within companies that contribute to poor service-quality perceptions by customers. Based on findings from the exploratory phase of our research, it develops a conceptual model linking customer-perceived quality deficiencies to within-company deficiencies or gaps. After discussing the conceptual model, the chapter outlines two additional research phases focusing on within-company gaps. Subsequent chapters discuss the findings from these two research phases and suggest remedial actions for closing the gaps.

EXPLORATORY EXECUTIVE STUDY

To gain insights about executives' views on what constitutes quality of service, we conducted a series of in-depth, face-to-face interviews as part of our exploratory research phase that included the customer focus-group interviews discussed in chapter 2. We interviewed executives from four nationally recognized companies chosen from the same four service sectors in which we conducted our customer focus group interviews; retail banking, credit cards, securities brokerage, and product repair and maintenance. The individuals we interviewed came from marketing, operations, customer relations, and senior management—areas in which executives should have a keen interest in service quality.

Our focus in the interviews was wide ranging. What did the executives perceive to be service-quality from the customers' perspective? Which key criteria did they believe their customers used in judging the quality of service provided by their companies? Which problems did they face in consistently delivering high-quality service? Which steps did they take to control or improve the quality of their services? Our dialogue with the executives provided us with a wealth of information concerning potential causes of service-quality shortfalls.

EXECUTIVE STUDY FINDINGS

As was true of the customer focus-group interviews, remarkably consistent patterns emerged from the four sets of executive interviews. Although some of the responses were specific to the companies and industries selected, most of the responses revealed common themes that cut across company and industry boundaries. These themes, which offer critical clues for achieving effective service-quality control, can be cast in the form of four key discrepancies or gaps pertaining to executive perceptions of service quality and the tasks associated with service delivery to customers. *These four gaps, which we define and discuss shortly, are the major causes of the service-quality gap customers may perceive* (i.e., the discrepancy between their expectations and perceptions as discussed in chapter 2).

To facilitate discussion of the various gaps, we denote the service-quality shortfall perceived by customers as Gap 5 and the shortfalls within the service provider's organization as Gaps 1 through 4. Because an aim of this chapter is to link the customer and provider gaps in the form of a conceptual framework for understanding and improving service quality, let us first review the diagram in exhibit 3–1 which represents Gap 5. (Exhibit 3–1 is an abbreviated version of exhibit 2–2.) As exhibit 3–1 shows, Gap 5 represents the potential discrepancy between the expected and perceived service from the customers' standpoint. Key determinants of the service expected by customers include word-of-mouth

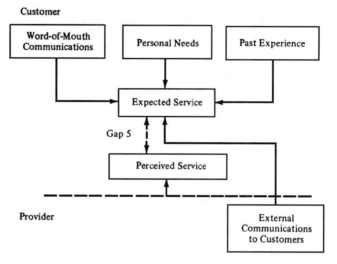

Exhibit 3–1 Gap 5: Between Customers' Expectations and Perceived Service

communications, personal needs, past experience, and external communications from the service provider. Next, we define and discuss each of the four service-provider gaps that contribute to Gap 5.

GAP 1: CUSTOMERS' EXPECTATIONS—MANAGEMENT-PERCEPTIONS GAP

In each of the four service sectors examined in our exploratory research, many of the executives' perceptions about what customers expect from superior quality service were congruent with the expectations expressed by customers themselves in the focus groups. Examples of attributes of quality service mentioned by both executives and customers include friendly and efficient bank tellers, error-free credit-card statements, honest securities brokers who have their customers' best interests at heart, and prompt repair of broken appliances. However, a number of discrepancies were also evident between expectations expressed by customers and executives' understanding of those expectations.

For example, privacy or confidentiality during transactions emerged as a pivotal quality attribute in every banking and securities-brokerage focus group we conducted. Customers in our focus groups expressed concern that their sensitive discussions with bank personnel or stockbrokers could easily be overheard by others because the service provider's physical facilities were not designed to ensure privacy. Yet the bank and securities brokerage executives we talked to were apparently oblivious to the importance attached by customers to transaction privacy. Not once did customers' concern for privacy surface in the executive interviews as a key ingredient of service quality.

A second illustration concerns the physical and security features of credit cards (e.g., the likelihood that unauthorized people could use the cards) which generated substantial discussion in the customer focus-group interviews but did not surface as a critical quality attribute in the executive interviews. Likewise, several customers in the credit-card focus groups expressed a preference for lower credit limits and higher minimum payments, implying a desire for disincentives to spend. Yet the executive interviews did not evidence cognizance of the fact that not all credit-card customers desire high credit limits. In fact, when asked to list in order of importance the most critical dimensions of service quality from the customers' perspective, one executive named credit availability first and stated that it would be a "great disservice" if customers are not given a "big enough limit."

In the product-repair-and-maintenance sector, focus-group participants indicated that they were unlikely to view large, nationally known repair service firms as high-quality firms. They consistently touted the quality of small, independent repair firms as being exemplary because such firms were much more reliable and responsive to customers' concerns. In contrast, most executive comments indicated that the size of their company and their national network of repair facilities would signal strength from a quality standpoint. Ironically, even though we did not reveal the identity of the repair company participating in our research to focus-group participants, several of them brought its name up and stated that they would not like to do business with it because it was too big, uncaring, and impersonal.

As demonstrated by the preceding illustrations, service-firm executives may not always be completely aware of which characteristics connote high quality to customers. Managers may not know about certain service features critical to meeting customers' desires; or, even when aware of such features, they may not know which levels of performance customers desire along those features.

When senior executives with the authority and responsibility for setting priorities do not fully understand customers' service expectations, they may trigger a chain of bad decisions and suboptimal resource allocations that result in perceptions of poor service quality. One example of misplaced priorities stemming from an inaccurate understanding of customers' expectations is spending far too much money on sprucing up the appearance of a company's physical facilities when customers may be much more concerned with how convenient, comfortable, and functional the facilities are. Another example is focusing training programs for contact personnel almost exclusively on the internal aspects of their jobs (e.g., filling out paperwork, following company rules and regulations) with little or no emphasis on aspects likely to be of greater concern to customers (e.g., answering customers' questions patiently and reassuringly, explaining the service to customers). The upshot is that senior managers' inaccurate understanding of what customers expect and what really matters to them, diagrammed as Gap 1 exhibit 3–2, is likely to result in service-delivery performance that is perceived by customers as falling short of their expectations (Gap 5). The necessary first step in improving quality of service (i.e., narrowing Gap 5) is for management to acquire accurate information about customers' expectations (i.e., close Gap 1).

GAP 2: MANAGEMENT'S PERCEPTIONS–SERVICE-QUALITY SPECIFICATIONS GAP

Management's correct perceptions of customers' expectations is necessary, but not sufficient, for achieving superior quality service. Another prerequisite for providing high service quality is the presence of performance standards mirroring management's perceptions of customers' expectations. However, a recurring theme that emerged from our executive interviews was the difficulty the executives experienced in translating their understanding of customers' expectations into service-quality specifications.

As we mentioned earlier, our exploratory research revealed a number

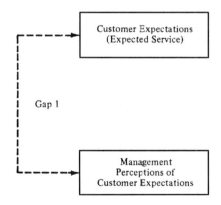

Exhibit 3–2 Gap 1: Between Customers' Expectations and Management's Perceptions of those Expectations

of areas of congruence between characteristics customers considered as indicators of high-quality service and those executives believed were critical to customers. In most of these instances, the executives had not converted their knowledge of customers' expectations into concrete performance standards. They cited a variety of constraints they believed to be insurmountable hurdles in setting service specifications consistent with customers' expectations. For instance, all the repair firm executives we interviewed were acutely aware that customers view rapid response to appliance breakdowns as a vital ingredient of high-quality service. Nonetheless, they found it difficult to establish precise performance standards for response time because of a lack of trained service personnel and wide fluctuations in customers' demand for service. As one executive observed, peak demand for repairing air conditioners and lawn mowers occurs during summer months, just as most service personnel want to go on vacations.

The apparent sense of frustration evident in the preceding example is also likely to be experienced by executives in other companies who believe that setting standards to deliver to certain customers' expectations is simply impossible. Their belief may stem from a variety of assumptions; for example, customers' expectations are unreasonable, the degree of variability inherent in the service defies standardization, the demand for the service is too hard to predict, the way the company and its personnel operate cannot be changed. Although some of these assumptions may be valid in some situations, whether they are legitimate long-term constraints that are impossible to overcome is questionable. Such assumptions may merely be rationalizations for management's reluctance to tackle head-on the difficult challenge of setting service standards.

In fact, the real reason for the potential gap between awareness of customers' expectations and the translation of that awareness into appropriate service standards may be the absence of wholehearted management commitment to service quality. David Garvin, after completing an extensive field study on goods quality, observed: "the seriousness management attached to quality problems [varies]. It's one thing to say you believe in defect-free products, but quite another to take time out from a busy schedule to act on that belief and stay informed."[1] Garvin's observations about good-producing companies clearly apply to service companies as well, particularly in view of the greater difficulty associated with achieving effective service-quality control.

While many service executives believe that it is impossible to set precise service specifications, a few companies have shown such a belief to be erroneous. National Westminster Bank USA is a case in point. Nat West set performance standards for its employees and also communicated those standards to customers in the form of performance guarantees in a series of creative television commercials called Raising the Standards of Banking. One commercial promised customers an immediate payment of $5 if they were displeased with the way they were greeted by a Nat West employee. Another commercial promised to pay customers $50 if their personal loan applications were not responded to by 5:00 P.M. the following day. Impressively, Nat West had to pay just two customer claims in the first six months of the campaign. According to Howard Deutsch, senior vice president/division head for quality improvement at Nat West, "By setting high service standards and putting our money where our mouth is, we're doing more than simply talking quality service. . . . We're guaranteeing it."[2]

Although perceived resource and market constraints, coupled with management indifference, may lead to Gap 2 (diagrammed in exhibit 3–3), this is a gap that can be closed effectively as demonstrated by Nat West. The quality of service delivered by customer-contact personnel is critically influenced by the standards against which they are evaluated and compensated. Standards signal to contact personnel what management's priorities are and which types of performance really count. When service standards are absent or when the standards in place do not reflect customers' expectations (e.g., when directory-assistance telephone operators are judged solely on the number of calls they handle per day) quality of service as perceived by customers is likely to suffer. In contrast, when

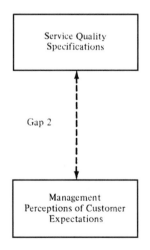

Exhibit 3–3 Gap 2: Between Management's Perceptions of Customers' Expectations and Service Quality Specifications

there are standards reflecting what customers expect (e.g., courteous treatment, quick response, and fulfilled promises as in the case of Nat West) the quality of service they receive is likely to be enhanced. Therefore, closing Gap 2—by setting performance standards that reflect customers' expectations—should have a favorable impact on customers' service-quality perceptions (Gap 5).

GAP 3: SERVICE-QUALITY SPECIFICATIONS—SERVICE-DELIVERY GAP

Each of the four companies that we examined did have some specifications for maintaining high service quality. The securities brokerage company, for example, required its customer-contact personnel to answer 90 percent of the phone calls from customers within ten seconds. This company also had a standard for keeping error rates in transactions within 1 percent. However, the executives we interviewed in this company (as well as in the other three companies) invariably expressed frustration at the inability of their employees to meet these service-performance standards.

Executives mentioned a variety of reasons for the discrepancy between service-performance standards and actual service delivery (i.e., Gap 3 depicted in exhibit 3–4). Most of these reasons pertain to the unwillingness and/or inability to contact personnel to meet the standards. When asked what caused service-quality problems in their companies, executives consistently mentioned the pivotal role of contact personnel. In the

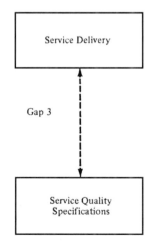

Exhibit 3–4 Gap 3: Between Service-Quality Specifications and Service Delivery

repair and maintenance company, for instance, one executive's immediate response to the source of service-quality problems was "Everything involves a person—a repair person. It's so hard to maintain standardized quality."

A stock-brokerage executive, anguishing over his company's inability to keep transaction error rates within the specified 1 percent, lamented: "I can handle 1 percent of 1,000 transactions but 1 percent of 300,000 transactions is another matter . . . [because] *blowout*—when the system stops working—may be close." In this instance, even though a performance standard was in place, meeting the standard was no longer possible because the volume of transactions had far outstripped existing capacity to process them accurately. Executives in the other companies also gave similar examples of service-performance shortfalls due to sheer increases in service loads without commensurate increases in capacity to serve.

Clearly then, even when guidelines exist for performing services well and treating customers correctly, high-quality service performance is not a certainty. A service-performance gap (Gap 3) is still likely due to a number of constraints (e.g., poorly qualified employees, inadequate internal systems to support contact personnel, insufficient capacity to serve). To be effective, service standards must not only reflect customers' expectations but also be backed up by adequate and appropriate resources (people, systems, technology). Standards must also be enforced to be effective—that is, employees must be measured and compensated on the basis of performance along those standards. Thus, even when standards accurately reflect customers' expectations, if management fails to "give teeth" to them—if it does not facilitate, encourage, and require their achievement—standards do no good. When the level of service-delivery performance falls short of the standards (Gap 3), it falls short of what customers expect as well (Gap 5). The implied direct association between Gaps 3 and 5 suggests that narrowing Gap 3—by ensuring that all the resources needed to achieve the standards are in place—should also reduce Gap 5.

GAP 4: SERVICE DELIVERY—EXTERNAL COMMUNICATIONS GAP

As we mentioned earlier, a key determinant of customers' expectations is the service provider's external communications (see exhibit 3–1). Promises made by a service company through its media advertising, sales force, and other communications raise expectations which serve as the standard against which customers assess service quality. A discrepancy between the actual service and the promised service (i.e., Gap 4 depicted in exhibit

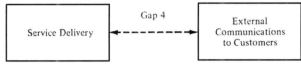

Exhibit 3–5 Gap 4: Between Service Delivery and External Communications to Customers about Service Delivery

3–5) therefore has an adverse effect on customers' perceptions of service quality (i.e., Gap 5). Customers who participated in our focus groups described many instances of poor service quality because of broken promises. A case in point is the following experience of a repair focus-group participant in her own words: "When I called [the repair company] for an appointment to come fix my washing machine they said that mine would be first call the next morning. . . . I took the next morning off from work and waited . . . and waited. . . . Finally at noon *I* called *them* and asked when their day began!"

Several of the executives we interviewed also described instances of broken promises because of inadequate coordination between operations and marketing. For instance, when the bank participating in our study introduced a new student-loan program, the marketing arm of the bank sold too many of the loans too fast without verifying in advance whether the operations group was geared up to mail out the loan checks as promised. Not surprisingly, broken promises and irate customers were the result. During the month following the introduction of the loan service the bank received over five hundred complaint letters from frustrated customers asking, "Where's my check?"

In addition to unduly elevating expectations through exaggerated claims, the executive interviews suggested another less obvious way in which external communications could influence customers' service-quality assessments. Some of the executives suggested that customers are not always aware of everything done behind the scenes to serve them well. By neglecting to inform customers of such behind-the-scenes efforts, companies may be forgoing an opportunity to favorably influence customers' service *perceptions*.

For instance, the securities-brokerage company had a "48-hour-rule" prohibiting its account executives from buying or selling securities for their personal accounts for the first 48 hours after information about the securities was supplied by the company. The brokers could advise clients and buy or sell on their behalf right away but they had to wait 48 hours before buying or selling for their own accounts. The company did not communicate this information to its customers, perhaps contributing to a perception that "all the good deals are probably made by the brokers for themselves" (a perception which surfaced in the securities-brokerage focus groups). One bank executive indicated that customers were unaware of the bank's behind-the-counter, on-line teller terminals which would "translate into visible effects on customer service." Making customers aware of hidden evidence of a company's commitment to quality service could improve customers' service perceptions. Customers who are aware that a company is taking concrete steps to serve their best interests are likely to perceive a delivered service in a more favorable way.

Customers' service perceptions may also be enhanced by educating customers to be better users of the service (e.g., telling brokerage customers the best times to call to check on their account status) and by adequately explaining to customers facets of the service process which they may consider to be irksome (e.g., why a customer ID is needed for certain bank transactions). Service companies frequently fail to capitalize on such opportunities to improve customers' perceptions. As one bank executive observed, "We don't teach our customers how to use us well and why we do the things we do."

In short, external communications can affect not only customers' expectations about a service but also customers' perceptions of the delivered service. Discrepancies between service delivery and external communications about it (Gap 4) adversely affect customers' assessment of service quality (Gap 5). Gap 4 essentially reflects an underlying breakdown in coordination between those responsible for delivering the service and those in charge of describing and/or promoting the service to customers. When the latter group of individuals do not fully understand the reality of the actual service delivery, they are likely to make exaggerated promises or fail to communicate to customers aspects of the service intended to serve them well. The result is poor service-quality perceptions. Effectively coordinating actual service delivery with external communications, therefore, narrows Gap 4 and hence favorably affects Gap 5 as well.

A SERVICE-QUALITY MODEL

The various gaps discussed thus far are the key ingredients in a recipe for gaining a good understanding of service quality and its determinants. Exhibit 3–6 shows how these ingredients can be combined to parsimoniously portray the provider's and customer's sides of the service-quality equation and the linkage between the two. The conceptual model in exhibit 3–6 conveys a clear message to managers wishing to improve

CUSTOMER

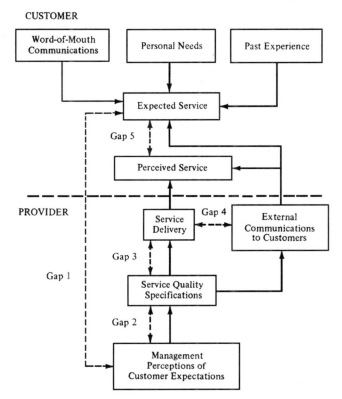

Exhibit 3–6 Conceptual Model of Service Quality

quality of service: The key to closing Gap 5 is to close Gaps 1 through 4 and keep them closed. To the extent that one or more of Gaps 1 through 4 exist, customers perceive service-quality shortfalls.

The conceptual model in exhibit 3–6 also implies a logical process which companies can employ to measure and improve quality of service. This process is diagrammed in exhibit 3–7. The sequence of questions in the five boxes on the left side of exhibit 3–7 correspond to the five gaps embedded in the conceptual model in exhibit 3–6. Specifically, the process begins with gaining an understanding of the nature and extent of Gap 5 and then successively searching for evidence of Gaps 1 through 4, taking corrective action wherever necessary.

Which factors are potential causes underlying the internal gaps (Gaps 1 through 4)? Which corrective actions are available to eliminate those causal factors? How can a company quantify the size of each gap and the extent to which the causal factors are contributing to it? To address these and other related issues, we undertook two additional research studies:

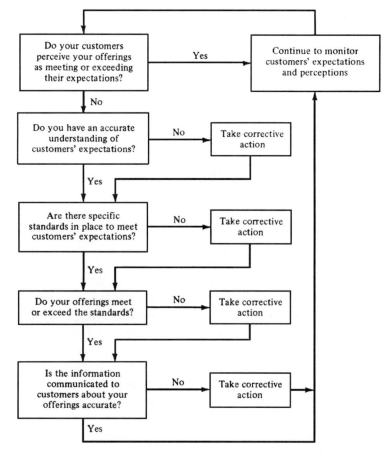

Exhibit 3-7 Process Model for Continuous Measurement and Improvement of Service Quality

(1) an in-depth study to uncover and understand potential antecedents of the four gaps; and (2) an empirical study to measure the relative sizes of the gaps and their antecedents. A description of these studies is given in "Additional Studies on Gaps 1–4." Findings from these studies and their implications are the focus of chapters 4 through 7.

SUMMARY

In this chapter we discussed our findings from exploratory qualitative research with senior executives; these findings were instrumental in our development of the service-quality-gap model. The findings revealed four key internal shortfalls or gaps that could contribute to poor quality of service as perceived by customers:

ADDITIONAL STUDIES ON GAPS 1 THROUGH 4

In-Depth Study

Building on what we had learned about the four internal gaps from our exploratory executive study, we conducted a comprehensive case study of a nationally known bank. We selected three of the bank's regions (each of which had at least 12 branches) and interviewed managers and employees at various levels individually and in focus groups. Top and middle managers responded to open-ended questions about their perceptions of customers' expectations of service quality (Gap 1), service-quality standards set by the organization to deliver quality (Gap 2), and differences between standards set by management and the level of service actually delivered (Gap 3). We conducted seven focus-group interviews with tellers, customer-service representatives, lending personnel, and branch managers from the three regions to help identify factors contributing to Gaps 3 and 4. Finally, we interviewed bank managers whose responsibilities included customer communications (bank marketing, advertising, and consumer affairs executives) and the president and creative director of the bank's advertising agency to identify the factors responsible for Gap 4.

We next conducted a systematic group interview with 11 senior managers of six nationally known service firms (two full-service banks, two national insurance companies, and two national telephone companies) to verify and generalize the factors we identified as contributing to Gaps 1 through 4. We presented our conceptual model, explained the four gaps, and questioned the managers about the factors responsible for the gaps in their firms. We also presented and discussed lists of factors derived from the preceding stage of our study. The managers augmented the lists and evaluated the factors on the basis of experience in their industries and organizations.

We then combined insights gained from the various stages with those from relevant marketing and organizational behavior literature and developed a classification of the main factors responsible for each of the four gaps. Chapters 4 through 7 are organized around the key factors pertaining to each gap.

Empirical Study

To measure Gaps 1 through 4 and the extent to which their antecedents were contributing to them, we conducted a major empirical study. In this study we used mail surveys to collect data from customers, contact personnel, and managers of five nationally known service companies (two insurance companies, two banks, and one long-distance telephone company). In all, 1,936 customers, 728 contact personnel, and 231 managers responded to our surveys.

The customer survey included the SERVQUAL instrument and questions to measure the relative importance of the five service-quality dimensions. Appendix A contains the SERVQUAL instrument and outlines the procedure for computing SERVQUAL scores. The manager and contact personnel surveys included the expectations section of SERVQUAL and the questions to measure the relative importance of the five service-quality dimensions. (Respondents completed both these sections *the way they thought their customers would complete them.*) A comparison of managers' and contact personnel's responses to these sections with customers' responses to the matching sections on the customer survey yielded measures of Gap 1 (appendix B gives further details on the measurement of Gap 1). The manager and contact personnel surveys also included questions to directly assess the extent of Gaps 2 through 4 and to measure the factors identified by the in-depth study as contributing to the four internal gaps. Appendix B contains the questions used to measure the gaps and their antecedents and outlines the corresponding scoring procedures.

Gap 1, the discrepancy between customers' expectations and managements' perceptions of those expectations; Gap 2, the discrepancy between managements' perceptions of customers' expectations and service-quality specifications; Gap 3, the discrepancy between service-quality specifications and actual service delivery; and Gap 4, the discrepancy between actual service delivery and what is communicated to customers about it. We linked customer-perceived quality shortfalls (Gap 5) to these four gaps in the form of a conceptual model of service quality. The conceptual model serves as a concise framework for understanding, measuring, and improving service quality. This chapter also outlined additional studies that we conducted to identify potential causes of the four internal gaps and to empirically examine the association between the gaps and their proposed antecedents. These studies' findings form the basis for chapters 4 through 7.

4

◇ ◇ ◇

GAP 1:
NOT KNOWING WHAT
CUSTOMERS EXPECT

K NOWING WHAT CUSTOMERS EXPECT is the first and possibly most critical step in delivering quality service. Stated simply, providing services that customers perceive as excellent requires that a firm know what
customers expect. Being a little bit wrong about what customers want can
mean losing a customer's business when another company hits the target
exactly. Being a little bit wrong can mean expending money, time, and
other resources on things that don't count to customers. Being a little bit
wrong can even mean not surviving in a fiercely competitive market.

This chapter details the first gap in the service-quality model: the difference between what customers expect and what management perceives
they expect. Sometimes this gap occurs because companies overlook or
underestimate the need to fully understand customers' expectations. Despite a genuine interest in providing service quality, many companies miss
the mark by thinking inside out—they know what customers should want
and deliver that—rather than outside in. When this happens, companies
provide services that do not match customers' expectations: important features are left out and the levels of performance on features that are provided
are inadequate. Because services have few clearly defined and tangible cues,
Gap 1 may be considerably larger in service companies than it is in manufacturing firms.[1]

KEY REASONS FOR GAP 1

Our research focusing on the provider's side of the gaps model indicates that three conceptual factors contribute to Gap 1. These factors,

illustrated in exhibit 4–1, are (1) *lack of marketing research orientation*, evidenced by insufficient marketing research, inadequate use of research findings, and lack of interaction between management and customers; (2) *inadequate upward communication* from contact personnel to management; and (3) *too many levels of management* separating contact personnel from top managers. Exhibit 4–2 defines these factors and presents several specific issues pertaining to them. In this chapter, we describe the problems stemming from these factors and offer suggestions for dealing with them to close Gap 1. We then discuss empirical findings from our research pertaining to Gap 1 and the organizational factors contributing to it.

GAP 1 PROBLEM: INSUFFICIENT MARKETING RESEARCH

Many service firms are new to marketing research. In fact, many service organizations are new to everything about marketing, believing that the operations function is more critical to success in the business.[2] Banks that close their branch lobbies in midafternoon to facilitate balancing the day's transactions and that issue monthly statements designed without input from customers exemplify an operations orientation. An

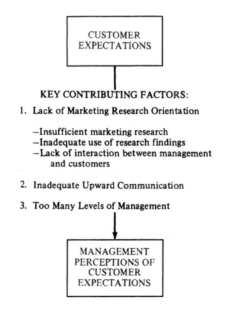

Exhibit 4–1 Key Factors Contributing to Gap 1

Factor and Definition	Specific Illustrative Issues
Marketing Research Orientation: Extent to which managers make an effort to understand customers' needs and expectations through formal and informal information-gathering activities.	· Is research conducted regularly to generate information about what customers want? · Does the marketing research a company conducts focus on quality of service delivered by it? · Do managers understand and utilize the research findings? · Do managers mingle with customers to learn what is on their minds?
Upward Communication: Extent to which top management seeks, stimulates, and facilitates the flow of information from employees at lower levels.	· Do managers encourage suggestions from customer contact personnel concerning quality of service? · Are there formal or informal opportunities for customer contact personnel to communicate with management? · How frequently do managers have face-to-face contact with customer contact personnel?
Levels of Management: Number of managerial levels between the topmost and bottommost positions.	· Do too many managerial levels separate top managers from those responsible for dealing with and serving customers?

Exhibit 4-2 Conceptual Factors Pertaining to Gap 1

operations orientation diverts focus from customers and reduces efforts to understand their needs and expectations.

Because marketing research is a key vehicle for understanding customers' expectations and perceptions of services, a firm that does not collect this information is more than likely to have a large Gap 1. A firm that does marketing research, but not on the topic of customers' expectations, may also have a large Gap 1. To close this gap, marketing research must focus on service quality issues such as which features are most important to customers, which levels of these features customers expect, and what customers think the company can and should do when problems occur in service delivery.

CLOSING GAP 1: RESEARCHING
CUSTOMERS' EXPECTATIONS

Finding out what customers expect is essential to providing service quality. Even when a service firm is small and has limited resources to conduct research, avenues are open to explore what customers expect. In exhibit 4–3 and in the discussion that follows, we present selected methods of researching customers' expectations beginning with the simplest (and least expensive) and ending with the most comprehensive (and often most costly) marketing research strategies.

USING COMPLAINTS STRATEGICALLY

Many companies depend solely on customers' complaints to stay in touch. Unfortunately, research conducted by TARP, a Washington, D. C., research organization has provided convincing evidence that customers' complaints are a woefully inadequate source of information: only 4 percent of customers with problems actually complain to companies. The other 96 percent stay dissatisfied, telling an average of nine to ten other people of their dissatisfaction.[3]

Even though listening to complaints is rarely sufficient to understand customers' expectations, complaints can become part of a larger process of staying in touch with customers. In particular, they can provide important information about the failures or breakdowns in the service system. If compiled, analyzed, and fed back to employees who can correct the problems, complaints can become an inexpensive and continuous source of adjustment for the service process.

L. L. Bean, for example, tracks complaints by product, tallying and summarizing them daily, and places them in a problem file accessible to all employees. The approach allows top management to review the key areas of customers' dissatisfaction on a regular basis, and to make changes swiftly to meet customers' expectations. Customer-service representatives are also able to act knowledgeably and helpfully when providing service to customers.[4]

Complaints also offer opportunities for managers and contact personnel to interact with customers, thereby learning detailed and rich information about products and services. Although a goods firm, Procter & Gamble Company recognizes the strategic advantages of providing service in the form of an 800-number that customers can call with problems. Through the telephone interaction, customer-service personnel ask specific questions, get to the heart of customers' problems, and learn more

Comp

—3 Selected Methods for Understanding Customers' Expectations

	Investment of Money	Investment of Time	Primary Uses
Strategic use of complaints	Low	Low	Identifying problems in the service process
Customers' desires in similar industries	Low	Low	Developing an initial framework for customers' expectations in focal industry
Research on intermediate customers	Moderate	Moderate	Efficient way to gain in-depth information on end customers
Key client studies	Moderate	Moderate	In-depth information on most important customers
Customer panels	Moderate to high	Moderate to high	Continuous source of information on changing customers' expectations
Transaction-based studies	Moderate	Moderate	Provides feedback on service-quality performance of each component of service quality.
Comprehensive customers' expectations studies	High	High	Establishes measures that are customer-based; provides foundation for tracking studies which provide a dynamic view of customers' expectations and perceptions

about the company's products. This information is then summarized and given to management as input when planning product or marketing changes.[5] Senior vice-presidents also spend three hours a week answering the phone, hearing customers' firsthand, answering questions, and addressing problems that are raised. Describing the value of the experience, one executive said, "I can't tell you what I do differently as a result of answering the phone, but I can tell you that no decision is made quite the same way."[6]

To truly understand customers' needs, companies can encourage and facilitate customers' feedback about problems. British Airways, for example, installed customer-complaint booths at Heathrow Airport where disgruntled passengers could air their grievances on videotape. Besides giving customers immediate relief from their annoyances, British Air found that the complaint videotapes gave vivid information to management about customers' problems and expectations.[7]

RESEARCHING WHAT CUSTOMERS WANT IN SIMILAR INDUSTRIES

As we discussed in chapter 2, our research revealed that customers have service expectations on dimensions that are similar across many industries. The five dimensions of quality service are the same across industries, and sometimes the way these dimensions are manifest is also similar across industries. Hospital patients and customers of hotels, for example, expect many of the same features when using these two services. Besides expert medical care, patients in hospitals expect comfortable rooms, courteous staff, and food that tastes good—the same features salient to hotel customers. In these and other industries that share common customers' expectations, managers may find it helpful to seek knowledge from executives in these other service industries. Because hotels have used marketing and marketing research longer than hospitals have, insights about hotel guests' expectations can inform about patients' expectations. Hospital administrators at Albert Einstein Medical Center in Philadelphia, for example, asked a group of nine local hotel executives for advice in understanding and handling patients. Many improvements resulted, including better food, easier-to-read name tags, more prominent information desks, and radios in many rooms.[8]

RESEARCHING INTERMEDIATE CUSTOMERS

Intermediate customers, such as contact employees, dealers, distributors, agents, or brokers, are people the company serves who serve the end customers. Researching the needs and expectations of these customers can be a useful and efficient way to obtain information about end users.

One way to research intermediate customers is to provide a service to them, such as education or training, then learn about their customers (and your own end customers) in the process. The interaction with intermediate customers provides opportunities for understanding end customers' expectations and problems. It can also help the company learn about and satisfy the service expectations of intermediate customers, a process critical in their providing quality service to end customers.

CONDUCTING KEY-CLIENT STUDIES

When the firm sells to businesses or to intermediate customers, rather than to end customers, some clients are large and important enough to study individually and in depth. To General Electric Company's (GE) aerospace group, for example, key clients included the Army, Navy, Air Force, and several airframe and electronics companies. To fully understand these clients' needs, as well as the strengths and weaknesses of the aerospace group vis-à-vis its competitors, the GE group interviewed 600 customers at all management levels of these key clients.[9] In a similar but more extensive effort, IBM Corporation created a customer council comprised of its top 50 clients. The company and the council meet regularly to determine where IBM will go in configuring and redesigning computer architecture.

These in-depth research studies can also be appropriate for end customers when key clients, who are larger or more important than others, can be identified. Law firms, for example, could focus on clients involved in major cases, banks could study their top depositors or borrowers, and airlines could research key corporate clients.

CREATING CUSTOMER PANELS

Firms can use customer panels to represent large segments of end customers. J. Bildner and Son's, a company that owns specialty food stores in Manhattan, keeps in touch through a customer advisory panel composed of 15–20 customers randomly selected in the stores. The panel meets three or four times a year to talk about products and services.[10] Similarly, New York State Electric and Gas Corporation formed a customer advisory panel of 15–21 members to represent a cross section of its small user customers (e.g., farmers, homemakers, consumer education people, the elderly) to test and assess their needs.[11] These panels allow the company to receive regular and timely information from customers.

TRACKING SATISFACTION WITH INDIVIDUAL TRANSACTIONS

A research trend gaining in popularity in service businesses involves transaction-based customer surveys. In this method, customers are surveyed immediately after a particular transaction about their satisfaction with the contact personnel with whom they interacted. Immediately after Sears, Roebuck & Company employees deliver furniture to homes—after they assemble the products, if necessary—they ask customers to complete five-item surveys measuring helpfulness, friendliness, and professionalism. Immediately after American Express customer-service representatives handle billing problems, they mail customers surveys that measure employees' courtesy and competence, and the customers' overall satisfaction. This type of research is simple, fresh, and provides management with current information about interactions with customers. Further, the research allows management to associate service-quality performance with individual contact personnel so that high performance can be rewarded and low performance corrected. It also serves as an incentive for employees to provide better service because they understand how and when they are being evaluated.

ENGAGING IN COMPREHENSIVE CUSTOMER-EXPECTATION STUDIES

Metropolitan Life Insurance Company of New York markets personal insurance to policyholders, group health and life coverage to corporations, and pension plans to both groups. The company developed a comprehensive program of measuring the expectations of all its customers, including both external and internal (employee) customers. According to John Falzon, senior vice-president of quality and planning, the importance of measuring service quality "applies equally across the board, not excluding internal customers. Maybe only 25 percent of our people are servicing an outside customer."[12]

Using companywide employee surveys, focus group interviews, and SERVQUAL, Met Life regularly monitors the expectations and perceptions of their customers. The 22-item generic SERVQUAL questionnaire, customized by adding questions covering specific aspects of service they wanted to track, formed the foundation for the comprehensive customer-expectation study.

The research strategy that American Express used to improve its service quality is another illustration of a comprehensive approach to understanding the needs and expectations of customers. The company sought and used input from as many sources as possible: customer research studies, customer complaints, employee surveys, and retailer studies. They found that customers were most concerned with *timeliness* (statements arriving at about the same time each month; address change corrections appearing quickly); *accuracy* (their names and addresses spelled correctly and bills accurate); and *responsiveness* (charges or payments reflected on their next statement). Through additional research, the company was able to establish the exact number of days that customers defined as responsive for the various company processes (e.g., two days for reissuing lost cards, 15 days for deciding on an application). Using this in-depth information, the company changed processes in the organization and tracked the changes in customers' perceptions that resulted.[13]

A comprehensive program works best when top management is dedicated to finding the truth about the company's customers. As an example, at Milliken and Company, the textiles company lauded for its customer service, the chairman spends 80 percent of his time "fathoming the needs of the customer." To support this mind-set, as he calls his dedication to customers, the company conducts extensive and detailed surveys to find whether and in which ways Milliken is responsive to them, researching all interactions including phone courtesy and billing.[14]

Customers' expectations change over time. As competition increases, as tastes change, and as customers become more knowledgeable, companies must continue to update their information and strategies. To stay in touch, New York State Electric and Gas Corporation continually monitors customers' desires through surveys, complaint analysis, focus groups, roundtables, customer panels, and face-to-face discussions with people in the organization.[15]

Recognizing that customers' expectations were dynamic, Merrill Lynch created a customer profiling and information system for "identifying client needs, updating these needs, and enabling account executives to match products to these needs."[16] Similarly, American Airlines Inc. used an ongoing in-flight survey to "ask our customers about their impressions of the ticket-buying process, the flight attendants, the gate agents—even the type of airplane they flew on."[17]

As shown in exhibit 4–3, the types of marketing research that we discuss in this section require different levels of investment and are appropriate for meeting slightly different service-quality objectives. We recommend a portfolio of these approaches designed to match each company's resources and to address the key areas needed to understand its customers. In chapter 8, we discuss this portfolio research approach in more detail.

GAP 1 PROBLEM: INADEQUATE USE OF MARKETING RESEARCH FINDINGS

Conducting marketing research is only the first part of understanding the customer. A service firm must also use the research findings in a meaningful way. The misuse or nonuse of research data can lead to a large gap in understanding customers' expectations. When managers do not read research reports because they are too busy dealing with the day-to-day challenges of the business, when they do not understand how to interpret the data because the research is too complex and technical, or when they lack confidence in the research, companies fail to use the resources available to them and Gap 1 widens. Understanding how to make the best use of research—to apply what they have learned to the business—is a key way to close Gap 1.

CLOSING GAP 1: USING MARKETING RESEARCH FINDINGS EFFECTIVELY

Managers must learn to turn research information and insights into action. The most comprehensive research does not help a company stay in touch unless the information gets to the right people in the firm in a timely manner. Consider the following examples of firms that have developed actionable research programs:

- Stew Leonard, of the much-acclaimed dairy store in Connecticut, believes that the suggestion box is the "pulse of the business." He empties it every day, compiles the list of recommendations, and distributes it to managers and employees. "Criticism and approval are taken to heart," says Leonard.[18]
- Goodyear Tire & Rubber Company conducts enough telephone interviews each week to obtain reliable information on customers' satisfaction with each of its 1,200 retail stores. When dissatisfied customers are identified, they are asked if they would like to be contacted by the store or district manager to address unresolved

complaints or problems. The company also follows some buyers up to two years to track their experiences, attitudes, and satisfaction. These results are compiled and regularly reported back to managers in marketing, production, and product development.[19]

• J. C. Penney Company, Inc., helps store managers understand and use research through a how-to bulletin. The bulletin advises them to ask shoppers leaving without packages questions to help them understand important service issues. The brochure also suggests guidelines about the optimal number (a minimum of 15 per week) and place (main entrance and within the store) for customer interviews. Ways to use customer feedback are emphasized.[20]

These examples illustrate creative and effective ways to use marketing research findings to improve quality of service. When management uses information, data, and findings from market research to understand customers' expectations, Gap 1 decreases.

GAP 1 PROBLEM: LACK OF INTERACTION
BETWEEN MANAGEMENT AND CUSTOMERS

In some service firms, especially ones that are small and localized, owners or managers may be in constant contact with customers, thereby gaining firsthand knowledge of customers' expectations and perceptions. But in large service organizations, managers do not always get the opportunity to experience firsthand what their customers want. This problem is illustrated in a comment from a bank's customer-service representative interviewed in an early stage of our research:

CUSTOMER-SERVICE REPRESENTATIVE: "We have three floors. Our manager, when he first got here, sat on the second floor. Now he is on the third floor in his enclosed office. He told us he doesn't want to be with the public. He needs time for himself. What are his priorities? He doesn't know what's going on on the first floor. I've had lots of customers ask for the manager. I say, 'I'm sorry, he's on a month's vacation.' "

The larger a company is, the more difficult it may be for managers to interact directly with customers and the less firsthand information they have about customers' expectations. Even when they read and digest research reports, managers can lose the reality of customers if they never get the opportunity to experience actual service. A theoretical view of how things are supposed to work cannot provide the richness of the service encounter. To truly understand customers' needs, management benefits from hands-on knowledge of what really happens in stores, on customer-service telephone lines, in service queues, and in face-to-face service encounters. If Gap 1 is to be closed, managers in large firms need some form of customer contact.

CLOSING GAP 1: INCREASING INTERACTION BETWEEN MANAGEMENT AND CUSTOMERS

Robert Crandall, CEO of American Airlines, illustrates the value in experiencing service firsthand.

> Commitment and dedication on the part of your people only happens when there's the same commitment and dedication on the part of the boss. Top management must confront the realities of the marketplace daily. I don't sit on some mountaintop, telling the American Airlines passenger service department how to deal with problems. I get out there and watch them work. I take regular trips on American—not because I have to go somewhere, but because I want to see for myself how we're doing.[21]

Managers can spend time on the line, interacting with customers and experiencing service delivery. A formal program for encouraging informal interaction is often the best way to ensure that the contact takes place. Radio Shack, for example, has a program called Adopt a Store through which senior managers spend time in stores collecting information and interacting with the staff.[22] Weinstock, a retailer in Sacramento, California, requires the entire headquarters staff to work the selling floor—in the trenches—seven times a year. "The plan was to give headquarters personnel hands-on knowledge of what really happens in stores, and not just a front office theoretical view of how things are supposed to work. What better way, the company reasoned, than to put central staff right in the trenches of selling?"[23]

The marketing director at Milliken called his experience working the swing shift "naive listening," and he described its benefits as follows:

> Getting close to the customer is a winner! . . . I worked the second shift (3:00 P.M. to midnight) and actually cleaned carpeting as well as hard-surface floors. I operated all the machinery they used daily, plus handled the same housekeeping problems. . . . Now I can put together my trade advertising as well as my entire merchandising

program based directly upon the needs of my customers as I observed them . . . I'm learning—from new-product introduction to maintenance of existing products—exactly what our health care customers require.[24]

As this example illustrates, direct interaction with customers adds clarity and depth to the manager's understanding of customers' expectations and needs.

GAP 1 PROBLEM: INSUFFICIENT UPWARD COMMUNICATION FROM CONTACT PERSONNEL TO MANAGEMENT

Customer-contact personnel are in regular contact with customers. Through this interaction, they come to understand a great deal about customers' expectations and perceptions. If the information they know can be passed on to top management, top managers' understanding of their customers may improve. In fact, it could be said that in many companies, top management's understanding of their customers depends largely on the extent and types of communication received from customer-contact personnel and from noncompany-contact personnel (e.g., independent insurance agents, retailers) who represent the company and its services. When these channels of communication are closed, management may not get feedback about problems encountered in service delivery and about how customers' expectations are changing.

In focus-group interviews conducted in one of our studies, several bank employees clearly illustrated the lack of effective upward communication.

BRANCH MANAGER: "I've been in this bank for 27 years and this is the first time I have had a regional VP that has never been in the branch."

ANOTHER: "He never will."

ANOTHER: "I haven't seen the man in a year and a half. That has a lot to do with our attitude. We're getting orders from someone we never see."

CLOSING GAP 1: IMPROVING UPWARD COMMUNICATION FROM CONTACT PERSONNEL TO MANAGEMENT

Sam Walton, founder of Wal-Mart, the highly successful discount retailer, once remarked, "Our best ideas come from delivery and stock boys."[25] To be sure he stays in touch with the source of new ideas, he spends considerable time in his stores working the floor, helping clerks or approving personal checks, even showing up at the loading dock with a bag of doughnuts for a surprised crew of workers.[26] "He would have his plane drop him next to a wheat field where he would meet a Wal-Mart truck driver. Giving his pilot instructions to meet him at another landing strip 200 miles down the road, he would make the trip with the Wal-Mart driver, listening to what he has to say about the company."[27]

Upward communication of this sort provides information to upper-level managers about activities and performances throughout the organization. Specific types of communication that may be relevant are formal (e.g., reports of problems and exceptions in service delivery) and informal (e.g., discussions between contact personnel and upper-level managers). Managers who stay close to their contact people benefit not only by keeping their employees happy but also by learning more about their customers.

Companies can use a variety of approaches for successfully achieving upward communication. For instance, Richard Rogers, president of Syntex Corporation, eats breakfast in the employee cafeteria every morning so he can be available to employees who want to see him.[28] Each year, Bill Marriott, Jr., visits 80 percent of the company's hotels, inspects a third of the flight kitchens, and eats at company restaurants as often as five times a week.[29] He is known for walking around his hotels at all hours, surveying breakfast preparations at 6: 15 A.M., or looking over rooms for the slightest imperfection.[30] Staying close to the customer is part of the Marriott tradition. William Marriott, Bill's father and Marriott's founder, is said to have read almost all of the customer comment cards for the entire 56 years of his leadership.[31]

Jim Kuhn, vice-president for individuality at McDonald's Corporation, sums up one reason why the fast-food company has been so successful: "We can never lose sight of the fact that this organization is run from the counter. A big part of the job is listening to the crew people."[32]

Companies such as McDonald's, Marriott, and Syntex encourage, appreciate, and reward upward communication from contact people. Through this important channel, management learns about customers' expectations from those employees in regular contact with customers and can thereby reduce the size of Gap 1.

GAP 1 PROBLEM: TOO MANY LEVELS BETWEEN CONTACT PERSONNEL AND MANAGEMENT

The number of managerial levels separating customer-contact personnel from top managers can affect the size of Gap 1. Multiple levels of management inhibit communication and understanding because they place barriers between top managers, who set standards for service quality, and contact people, who actually deliver quality to customers. As discussed in the previous section, Gap 1 can be reduced through upward communication from customer-contact personnel; this channel of communication becomes less effective the greater the number of levels because information is likely to be lost or misinterpreted in each translation from level to level. The greater the number of levels, the less likely that information employees possess about customers' expectations actually reaches managers. Therefore, the greater the number of levels between customer-contact personnel and top managers, the larger Gap 1 is likely to be.

CLOSING GAP 1: REDUCE THE NUMBER OF LEVELS BETWEEN CONTACT PERSONNEL AND MANAGEMENT

Many large organizations today are recognizing the value of reducing management levels that make companies sluggish and slow to adapt. IBM Corporation is removing managers from the middle and putting them in contact with customers, believing that the company must learn to react quickly and flexibly if it is to remain the leader in an increasingly competitive and dynamic computer market. IBM uses an approach it calls Best of Breed in which each area of the company identifies the competitor that best satisfies the expectations of a group of customers; then they set out to find out how to perform to that level. Only by eliminating unnecessary layers and teaching managers to focus on the outside—on customers and competitors—can the industry giant behave like a nimble, flexible company in all the markets it serves. Eliminating levels of management allows managers to be closer to customers, to understand their needs and expectations.

Milliken prides itself on having reduced the number of middle managers (called management associates) from 52,000 in 1981 to 31,000 in 1988. John Rampey, a senior executive and frequent spokesman for the company, claims that the more layers eliminated, the better the company understands the expectations of customers. He explains that remaining associates benefit from self-management and the creativity and problem solving that result from more direct interaction with the company. While removing the layers can be a painful process in the short term for employees, the long-term benefits of knowledge of customers, flexibility, and creativity make it worth the effort.

EMPIRICAL FINDINGS ABOUT GAP 1

A common piece of folk wisdom, and one that we implicitly invoked in discussing the importance of upward communication earlier in this chapter, holds that contact personnel, by virtue of their proximity to customers, understand customers' expectations better than managers understand them. In our empirical study of the five large service companies, we had an opportunity to evaluate the soundness of this folk wisdom. As described in our technical appendix B at the end of the book, we had customers complete the Servqual scale. Then we had contact personnel and managers fill out the expectations and dimensional-importance sections of Servqual as they perceived their customers would complete it.

Results of the comparison of these scores provides evidence that partially contradicts the folk wisdom. Exhibit 4–4 shows customers' expectations and contact personnel and managers' predictions of those expectations on the five dimensions of service quality. Reading across the rows, averages with similar letters indicate perceptions that are the same in a statistical sense. Different letters show that perceptions are statistically different.

On the dimension of tangibles, contact people were more accurate than managers in predicting customers' expectations. But in reliability, responsiveness, assurance, and the overall level of expectations, managers were significantly more accurate than contact personnel in predicting customers' expectations. These results suggest that managers understand customers' expectations better than contact personnel in the companies

Exhibit 4–4 Comparison of Customers' Expectations with Managers' and Contact Personnel's Perceptions of Those Expectations

	Customers	Contact Personnel	Managers
Tangibles	5.29[a]	5.50[b]	5.54[b]
Reliability	6.48[a]	6.09[b]	6.39[a]
Responsiveness	6.40[a]	6.12[b]	6.32[a]
Assurance	6.47[a]	6.27[b]	6.43[a]
Empathy	6.25[a]	5.96[b]	6.06[b]
Total	6.19[a]	6.00[b]	6.15[a]

* Reading across the rows, numbers with similar letters indicate perceptions that are statistically the same. Numbers with different letters indicate perceptions that are statistically different.

we studied. Whether or not these results would occur in other companies would depend on their managers' and contact personnel's understanding of customers' expectations and hence the size of Gap 1 for the two groups of employees. Procedures for measuring the status of Gap 1—as well as Gaps 2 through 4—in any company are discussed in appendix B.

As the preceding discussion and the evidence in exhibit 4–4 indicate, Gap 1 as defined in our service-quality model (i.e., the difference between customers' expectations and managers' perceptions of those expectations) was not a serious shortfall in the companies we studied. In fact, the *weighted expectation* scores—scores that capture not only the expectation levels along the SERVQUAL dimensions but also the relative importance of the dimensions themselves—for managers and customers were similar for all five companies. (The procedure for computing the weighted expectation scores is described in appendix B.) On the scale of 1 to 7 that we used to measure expectations, the weighted scores for the two groups were as follows:

	Managers	Customers
Company 1	6.4	6.3
Company 2	6.3	6.3
Company 3	6.3	6.3
Company 4	6.1	6.4
Company 5	6.0	6.4

Despite the relatively small Gap 1 in each of the five companies, our findings about the factors that could potentially result in Gap 1 revealed opportunities for improvement in each company. Exhibit 4–5 reports the average scores for the five companies on marketing research orientation, upward communication, and levels of management. These scores are on seven-point scales on which higher scores represent more favorable levels (further details about how these factors are measured are in appendix B). The discrepancy between each average score and a score of 7 (the highest possible score) represents the potential for improvement. The results for the five firms we studied imply that improvements can be made along all these factors. However, the perception that too many levels of management separate contact personnel from top management is a more significant problem than either a lack of marketing research orientation or

Exhibit 4–5 Scores on Factors Pertaining to Gap 1*

	Marketing Research Orientation	Upward Communication	Levels of Management
Company 1	5.3	4.7	3.3
Company 2	4.2	4.7	3.6
Company 3	4.3	4.4	3.8
Company 4	5.0	5.0	2.2
Company 5	4.7	4.4	2.3
All companies	4.7	4.6	3.0

* Scores are average values on a seven-point scale on which higher numbers represent more favorable scores.

inadequate upward communication. Indeed, the consistency of this finding across all five of our sample companies, coupled with our finding that top managers had a more accurate view of customers' expectations, suggest an intriguing hypothesis: In large companies, too many levels of management may be inhibiting *downward communication* from top management to contact personnel. The managerial sophistication and market knowledge of top decision makers in large companies apparently give them an accurate understanding of customers' expectations. Ironically, the multiple levels of management characteristic of many large companies may be significant hurdles in conveying top management knowledge about what customers expect down to the customer-contact personnel responsible for meeting customers' expectations. A rich reservoir of knowledge about customers' expectations does a company little good if it is blocked at the upper echelons of management. Top management must disseminate that knowledge to the lower levels by breaking down or working around intermediate barriers to effective downward communication.

SUMMARY

This chapter identified the key problems which result in Gap 1, a discrepancy between what customers expect and what management perceives that they expect. These problems include insufficient marketing research, inadequate use of marketing research findings, lack of interaction between management and customers, insufficient upward communication from contact employees to managers, and too many managerial levels between contact personnel and top management. We described each of these problems and discussed specific strategies and tactics for closing Gap 1. Finally, we presented empirical findings from our research pertaining to Gap 1 and its antecedents and explored the implications of these findings.

5

◇ ◇ ◇

GAP 2:
THE WRONG SERVICE-
QUALITY STANDARDS

A S DISCUSSED IN CHAPTER 4, understanding customers' expectations is
the first step in delivering high service quality. Once managers
accurately understand what customers expect, they face a second critical
challenge: using this knowledge to set service-quality standards for the
organization. Management may not be willing (or able) to put the systems
in place to match or exceed customers' expectations. A variety of factors—
including resource constraints, short-term profit orientation, market conditions, or management indifference—may account for Gap 2, the
discrepancy between managers' perceptions of customers' expectations
and the actual specifications they establish for service delivery.

Gap 2 is a wide gap in many companies. A recurring theme in the
executive interviews in our research was the difficulty experienced in
attempting to match or exceed customers' expectations. Many executives
cannot or will not change company systems of service delivery to enhance
customers' perceptions. Doing so often requires altering the very process
by which work is accomplished. At other times, change requires new
equipment or technology. Change also necessitates aligning executives
from different parts of the firm to collectively understand the big picture
of service quality from the customer's point of view. And almost always
change requires a willingness to be open to different ways of structuring,
calibrating, and monitoring the way service is provided.

In our extensive research on the gap constructs and measures (see
chapter 3 for details), we identified the four conceptual factors (shown in
exhibit 5–1 and described in exhibit 5–2 which result in the following
major reasons for Gap 2: (1) *inadequate commitment to service quality*, (2) *lack*

71

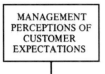

KEY CONTRIBUTING FACTORS:

1. Inadequate Management Commitment
   to Service Quality

2. Perception of Infeasibility

3. Inadequate Task Standardization

4. Absence of Goal Setting

Exhibit 5–1 Key Factors Contributing to Gap 2

of perception of feasibility, (3) *inadequate task standardization*, and (4) *absence of goal setting*. In this chapter, we discuss these reasons and offer suggestions on ways to overcome them. We conclude with a description of the empirical results from our research relating to Gap 2.

GAP 2 PROBLEM: INADEQUATE MANAGEMENT COMMITMENT TO SERVICE QUALITY

The absence of total management commitment to service quality virtually guarantees a wide Gap 2. Emphasis on other company performance objectives, such as cost reduction and short-term profit, is easier to measure and track; therefore it may supersede emphasis on service quality. The tendency on the part of executives to focus on other objectives is illustrated in the following statement by Arnoldo Hax and Nicolas Majluf, authors in the field of strategic management: "Most U.S. firms suffer significantly from the use of short-term accounting-driven measures of performance to establish the reward mechanisms for high-level managers, who are mainly responsible for implementing strategic actions."[1]

Louis Gerstner, former president of American Express, suggests another powerful explanation for lack of management commitment

Factor and Definition	Specific Illustrative Issues
Management Commitment to Service Quality: Extent to which management views service quality as a key strategic goal.	• Are resources committed to departments to improve service quality? • Do internal programs exist for improving the quality of service to customers? • Are managers who improve the quality of service to customers more likely to be rewarded than other managers? • Does the company emphasize its sales goals as much as or more than it emphasizes serving customers? • Are upper and middle managers committed to providing quality service to their customers?
Perception of Feasibility: Extent to which managers believe that customer expectations can be met.	• Does the company have the necessary capabilities to meet customer requirements for service? • Can customer expectations be met without hindering financial performance? • Do existing operations systems enable customer expectations to be met? • Are resources and personnel available to deliver the level of service that customers demand? • Does management change existing policies and procedures to meet the needs of customers?
Task Standardization: Extent to which hard and soft technology are used to standardize service tasks.	• Is automation used to achieve consistency in serving customers? • Are programs in place to improve operating procedures so that consistent service is provided?
Goal-Setting: Extent to which service quality goals are based on customer standards and expectations rather than company standards.	• Is there a formal process for setting quality of service goals for employees? • Does the company have clear goals about what it wants to accomplish? • Does the company measure its performance in meeting its service quality goals? • Are service quality goals based on customer-oriented standards rather than company-oriented standards?

Exhibit 5–2 Conceptual Factors Pertaining to Gap 2

to service quality. "Because of the structure of most companies, the guy who puts in the service operation and bears the expense doesn't get the benefit. It'll show up in marketing, even in new product development. But the benefit never shows up in his own P&L statement."[2]

Many companies believe they are committed to service quality but their commitment is to quality from the company's own internal, technical perspective. Service quality in many firms means meeting the company's self-defined productivity or efficiency standards, many of which customers do not notice or desire. In other firms, quality is defined in terms of advanced technology—meeting standards required to keep pace with competitors on things which customers will not pay for and do not want. In our view, being committed to service quality means more than meeting company- or competitor-defined standards. Management commitment to service quality means providing service that the *customer perceives as high in quality*, as expressed by James Robinson of American Express: "Overriding all other values is our dedication to quality. We are a market-driven institution, committed to our customers in everything we do. We constantly seek improvement and we encourage the unusual, even the iconoclastic."[3]

When managers are not committed to service quality *from the customer's point of view*, they target resources only to other organizational goals such as sales, profits, or market share. They do not establish internal service-quality initiatives, and they do not see that attempts to improve service quality lead to better company performance.

CLOSING GAP 2: COMMITTING TO QUALITY

Delivering quality service requires leadership and commitment from top management, a point we stressed in chapter 1. Without this commitment—this willingness to temporarily accept the difficulties involved in change—quality service simply does not happen. Contact employees and middle management do not and cannot improve quality without strong leadership from management. Strong management commitment and leadership is illustrated by a poster prominently displayed at L. L. Bean, the successful direct-mail marketer.

> What Is a Customer? A Customer is the most important person even in this office . . . in person or by mail. A Customer is not dependent on us . . . we are dependent on him. A Customer is not an interruption of our work . . . he is the purpose of it. We are not doing a favor by serving him . . . he is doing us a favor by giving

us the opportunity to do so. A Customer is not someone to argue or match wits with. Nobody ever won an argument with a Customer. A Customer is a person who brings us his wants. It is our job to handle them profitably to him and to ourselves.[4]

Among companies that sell to other businesses, rather than to end customers, stand those whose customer-oriented philosophies lead them to be the best in their fields. DuPont, the top-rated firm among chemical companies, captures the reason for its success simply: "Our marketing effort starts with the customer."[5]

Top managers committed to quality must constantly and visibly express their commitment to the troops. Stew Leonard, of the highly respected dairy store of the same name, demonstrates his commitment to his customers with a three-ton granite block at the store's entrance reading:

Rule 1: The customer is always right.

Rule 2: If the customer is ever wrong, reread rule 1.[6]

Bill Marriott, Jr., continues his father's legendary commitment to customers and visibly expresses it by traveling the country to personally oversee operations. He claims: "It's a commitment. I'm the first in and the last out. If you are a leader, you better lead—and you lead by example. You have to motivate people, let them know you want to see what they can do."[7]

CLOSING GAP 2: GAINING COMMITMENT OF MIDDLE MANAGEMENT

If top-management commitment is the key to setting service standards to deliver quality, middle-management commitment is the key to making those standards work. Lack of support from middle management can derail the service-quality journey. Middle management often feels worn down by the "program of the month" treadmill and has inadequate time and support to keep up. If middle management perceives that service quality is just another program of the month, resistance rather than support will ensue. If middle management doesn't pass along top management's commitment to quality by communicating service standards, by setting service standards for their work units, and by reinforcing the standards with motivation and support, quality service simply does not happen.

Middle management must see that their efforts toward service quality are being noticed and appreciated. Incentives for managerial participation and improvements must be provided. Financial incentives linked to behavior that fosters high service quality, in addition to more typical performance goals such as sales, make service quality real for them. In one of the service organizations that sponsored our research, top management instituted a new 60-40 bonus plan to support the company's quest for quality. Instead of managerial bonuses based 100 percent on sales, the company rewarded managers on both sales (60 percent) and service quality (40 percent).

Training in the skills needed to lead service workers to deliver quality is often necessary. In its effort to enlist middle management's support and involvement in service quality, British Airways developed a five-day management training course called Managing People First. The course's objectives were to "make managers more decisive and creative, more responsive to the needs and concerns of their staff and colleagues, and more effective in motivating their subordinates to use their own judgment and initiative."[8] The airline also linked direct financial incentives to managers' behaviors in achieving these objectives through a strategy they call the three-legged stool:

> The seat of the stool represents the British Airways way of managing. The first leg is the "Managing People First" training program; the second leg is an evaluation program designed to measure not only what managers achieve, but how; and the third leg is a compensation program, whereby managers receive lump-sum bonus payments up to 20% of base salary, determined by what the manager achieves and how.[9]

GAP 2 PROBLEM: PERCEPTION OF INFEASIBILITY

Our research revealed that the size of Gap 2 is strongly affected by the extent to which managers perceive that meeting customers' expectations is feasible. As we saw in chapter 3, executives in the repair service firm participating in our exploratory study were fully aware that customers view quick response to appliance breakdowns as a vital aspect of high-quality service. However, they believed that establishing specifications to deliver a quick response consistently was not feasible for two reasons: (1) the time required to provide a specific repair service was difficult to forecast; and (2) skilled service technicians were less available in the peak summer season than at any other time. In this and many other situations, knowledge of customers' expectations exists but the perceived means to deliver to expectations apparently do not.

Perception of infeasibility is a managerial mind-set that may or may not be related to actual constraints on the organization. It may be true that technology available to improve a service delivery system does not exist, that financial constraints preclude the manager from aligning the firm to serve all the needs of customers, and that some customers' expectations and demands are simply too rigid and unrealistic. In these cases, managers may have no choice but to decide that meeting customers' expectations is infeasible. In our research, however, we found that the perception of infeasibility is often the result of short-term, narrow thinking on the part of managers—an unwillingness to think creatively and optimistically about customers' needs, and an excuse for maintaining the status quo.

CLOSING GAP 2: CREATING POSSIBILITIES

Being open to innovation, being receptive to different and possibly better ways of doing business—thinking big—is the key to perceiving feasibility. Managers in truly successful service companies have the perception that almost anything the customer wants is feasible. These managers are willing to change the way they do business, if necessary, and to invest money, time, and effort to fully satisfy their customers.

When hotel customers repeatedly complained that they didn't like to wait in lines to check out, most hotels threw up their hands and said that the problem couldn't be helped. Bill Marriott, Jr., however, thought it important enough to devise an alternative way to handle this recurring and pivotal customer request: the company invented Express Checkout. Customers, especially those in a hurry, could simply drop their keys at the counter if their bills, which had been slipped under their doors during the night, were accurate. Companies such as Marriott constantly pioneer customer-service advancements because they view customers' demands as challenges and puzzles rather than as problems.

American Express Company's Travel-Related Services (TRS) division found customers' expectations about credit-card services increased tremendously as competition in the industry intensified. Rather than accept performance that departed more and more from expectations as the competitive pressure built, the company decided that computer improvements were the answer to meeting customers' expectations. Through the computer improvements TRS developed, many important customer requests were met. The division reduced personal card processing from an average of 35 days to 15 days, replaced cards in an average of 2 days rather than 15 days, dropped response time to cardholder inquiries from 16 to 10 days, answered merchant inquiries in 4 days rather than 14, and reduced emergency service for card replacement to within 24 hours worldwide.[10]

American Airlines is another successful service company known for its innovative solutions to difficult service challenges. Over the years the airline has developed major service innovations that include in-flight entertainment, one-stop check-in, advance boarding passes, and automated reservations.[11] With the confusion and complexity that accompanied deregulation, American made the decision that the only way travel agents could cope was with computers. It responded by developing Sabre, a $200 million automated reservation system that revolutionized the industry. As an American executive explains:

> Most people think of Sabre as a computerized reservations system, and it is, but it also is much more than that. Sabre is a powerful, integrated data processing and communications system. It contains schedules for nearly 600 airlines. It has information on rental cars, hotels, broadway plays and foreign currency exchange rates. It lets travel agents sell their clients such things as flowers by wire, insurance and telex message capability.[12]

Another perplexing service problem involves the impact of weather on overnight mail delivery. Firms such as Airborne Express, Federal Express Corporation, and United Parcel Service set service standards and typically meet them as long as the weather is good. But customers want reliable, on-time, overnight delivery service even when weather makes delivery difficult or impossible. Most delivery companies settled for doing their best to adapt to weather, but Federal Express created possibilities by designing "nowcasting," a weather assessment and forecasting tool. Nowcasting assists its employees in achieving on-time performance no matter what the weather and provides "the most up-do-date, specific weather data to enable Federal Express to make contingency plans for its chief function: safe delivery of packages."[13]

Companies that create possibilities actively look for ways to provide better service to customers. Knowing that the detail involved in ordering supplies for hospitals can be overwhelming to customers, American Hospital Supply Corporation sought to turn this customer problem into a competitive advantage. The company developed an easier, customer-oriented ordering process by providing computer terminals to customers from which they could order all medical supplies quickly and conveniently. Customers were satisfied and the system made switching to a rival difficult; once customers were familiar with the computer system, the effort and learning cost of changing suppliers was high.[14]

Computer information systems are often the basis for setting standards to improve customer service. L. L. Bean, the direct marketer, earned its reputation for outstanding customer service using a computer data base that supplies moment-to-moment information about models, colors, and sizes of products in stock. With this system, the company can set and achieve high standards of customer service. The data base enables them to fill an incredible 99.8 percent of orders accurately.[15]

Marshall Field & Company uses a computer information system to deal with the difficult problem of scheduling employees. Having enough employees on the floor to serve customers well while not wasting resources is an ongoing challenge for large retail stores. Marshall Field developed a computer-based employee scheduling system to "maximize sales potential at point-of-sale, increase managerial effectiveness, and improve expense and productivity controls," all while setting high standards for service provided to customers. Using a personal computer, the company developed a program using as data daily sales plans by department, customer traffic patterns, store hours, company meal and break policies, and employee schedule availability. The computer generated weekly employee schedules with the right number of salespeople on duty at peak selling periods, even if that meant bringing extra help in to meet the levels of service the company wanted to provide its customers.[16]

All of these examples illustrate different approaches to creating possibilities, ways to provide the quality service customers expect.

GAP 2 PROBLEM: INADEQUATE STANDARDIZATION OF TASKS

The translation of managerial perceptions into specific service-quality standards depends on the degree to which tasks to be performed can be standardized or routinized. Some executives and managers believe that services cannot be standardized—that customization is essential for providing high-quality service. Somehow, standardizing tasks is perceived as being impersonal, inadequate, and not in the customer's best interests. Further, they feel that services are too intangible to be measured. This view leads to vague and loose standard setting with little or no measurement or feedback.

In reality, many service tasks are routine (such as those needed for opening checking accounts or spraying lawns for insects), and for these, specific rules and standards can be fairly easily established and effectively executed. If services are customized for individual customers (e.g., investment portfolio management or estate planning), specific standards (such as those relating to time spent with the customer) seem more difficult to establish. Even in highly customized services, however, some aspects of service provision can be routinized. Physicians and dentists, for example, can and do standardize recurring and nontechnical aspects of the service such as checking patients in, collecting payments, weighing patients, and taking temperatures. In delegating these routine tasks to assistants, physicians and dentists can spend more of their time on the more expert services of diagnosis or patient care.

CLOSING GAP 2: STANDARDIZING TASKS

According to Harvard's Ted Levitt, a long-time observer of service industries, standardization of service can take three forms: (1) substitution of hard technology for personal contact and human effort; (2) improvement in work methods or soft technology; and (3) combinations of these two methods.[17] Examples of hard technology include automatic teller machines, automatic car washes, and airport X-ray machines, all of which allow standardization of service provision by substituting machines for human effort. Soft technology is illustrated by restaurant salad bars and routinized tax and accounting services developed by firms such as H & R Block, Inc., and Comprehensive Accounting Corporation.

Hard and soft technologies facilitate the standardization of service necessary to provide consistent delivery to customers. By breaking tasks down and providing them efficiently, hard technology allows the firm to calibrate service standards such as the length of time a transaction takes, the accuracy with which operations are performed, and the number of problems that occur. In developing soft technology, the firm comes to understand completely the process by which the service is delivered; with this understanding, the firm more easily sets service standards.

CLOSING GAP 2 WITH HARD TECHNOLOGY

Hard technology can simplify and improve customer service, particularly when it frees company personnel by handling routine, repetitious tasks and transactions. Customer-service employees can then spend more time on the personal and possibly more essential portions of the job. American Airlines, whose standardized and automated baggage handling process is legendary, learned long ago that the standardization of its baggage system with hard technology could free the company to provide highly personalized service.

> A phone call to the lost-baggage number from any location at any hour is answered by a live sales rep at a center manned around the clock. The live voice didn't know any more than the tape message did but the reality was the sympathetic response the living person provided—a degree of comfort no tape machine could match.[18]

Some hard technology, in particular computer data bases that contain information on individual needs and interests of customers, allows the company to standardize the essential elements of service delivery. Basic delivery standards can then be established and measured. Some types of hard technology useful in standard setting include information data bases, automated transactions, and scheduling and delivery systems. Effective use of these types of technology is illustrated in the following company examples:

Information Data Bases. Campbell Soup Company receives regular requests for information about product ingredients, nutritional value, and flavors. Because many of these requests are repetitious, the company created a large computer data base to respond to these special requests. The data base allows Campbell to define service protocols, standard ways to respond quickly to customer requests, appearing to give individualized attention and answers to all questions. The data base frees up employees, as the only questions that must be handled personally by staff members are those that do not fall into the categories covered by the data base.[19]

Automating Tasks. Marshall Field eliminated "task-interfering duties" for salespeople. The retail store automated check approval, implemented in-store telephone directors to allow employees to contact other departments and other stores quickly, reorganized wrapping stations, and simplified order forms, all of which resulted in faster checkout and more attention to customers.[20] Each of these tasks had previously required varying amounts of time and blocked employees from responding quickly to customers' requests. With the new system, standards for service could be established and employees could quickly handle these simple tasks.

Scheduling and Delivery Systems. Pizza Hut centralized and computerized its home-delivery operations. Rather than having the separate tasks of order taking, baking, and delivery all in the same location, the company developed a system that works more effectively for both the company and its customers. Operators in a customer-service center (not a bakery) take requests for pizza. Working from a data base that shows past orders, trained operators take an average of 17 seconds to verify directions to a caller's home and enter his or her request. Operators then route the orders to the closest bake shops, which are strategically located throughout cities to ensure fast deliveries. Cooks in the satellite bakeshops prepare pizzas on instructions sent to bakeshop printers from order-takers' computers. Drivers aim to complete their deliveries within a half-hour of a customer's call and usually succeed.[21]

CLOSING GAP 2 WITH SOFT TECHNOLOGY: CHANGING THE WORK PROCESS

Standardizing some aspects of the service process is often desirable in providing consistent service quality. Mini-Maids Services, a firm that franchises home and office janitorial services, has successfully built a business by developing a repertoire of 22 standard daily cleaning chores. The company sends out crews of four who perform these 22 tasks in an average time of 55 minutes for a fee of $39.50 to $49.50.[22]

How does a company change the way work is done to gain these types of internal efficiencies without sacrificing perceived service quality? American Express's service-quality approach is an ideal illustration of the process. It "had all the earmarks of a classic industrial engineering study. It broke operations into discrete elements, measured how long each one took, set performance standards, and devised ways of meeting them."[23] First, the company defined four customer categories: traveler's-check purchasers, check sellers (banks), merchants who accept checks, and refund agents who reimburse the merchants. More than 100 managers from these areas joined with quality staffers to specify 50 separate services provided to these customers. Next, they determined how long these tasks were taking at the time and the ideal amount of time from their customers' perspectives. When these two measurements (present amount of time and ideal amount of time) differed, smaller groups of employees devised methods to improve them. As an example, by designing 13 new form letters and batching similar correspondence to help the word processing center better organize its workload,[24] response time to cardholders' written inquiries was cut to from 16 to 10 days.

When service to customers involves several different departments or areas in the firm, the company must link them together in meaningful ways from its customers' point of view. Merrill Lynch & Company designed a system called the Critical Path to track work as it passed through the company:

> Getting new products launched successfully requires many areas of the firm to work together. So we are standardizing the product introduction process . . . a checklist was designed so everyone knows what's needed and has adequate lead time to do their job. This checklist was administered by the New Product Committee . . . a Marketing Calendar was created and is being published monthly in an internal, management newsletter.[25]

Another important advantage to standardizing routine transactions is that the firm can free resources to personalize and improve service to its best customers. For this approach to work, the company must first define those best customers through criteria that make them easy to access. As an example, the Marriott Corporation defined as an Honored Guest those customers who spend at least 15 nights at a Marriott hotel or resort over a 12-month period. Guests who meet these qualifications receive service enhancements, amenities, and other benefits. The best Honored Guests, those who spend at least 75 nights over a 12-month period at a Marriott hotel or resort, receive the top treatment: an upgrade to a suite or concierge-level guestroom, direct billing, a room-service gift and a welcome note from the general manager. These special guests do not feel they are receiving treatment that is standardized, yet it is: Honored Guests get standard special treatment.[26]

Standardization, whether accomplished by hard or soft technology, reduces Gap 2. Both technology and improved work processes structure important elements of service provision. The process of standardization facilitates goal setting, which we discuss in the next section.

GAP 2 PROBLEM: ABSENCE OF GOAL SETTING

Companies that have been successful in delivering consistently high service quality are noted for establishing goals or standards to guide their employees in providing service quality. Of critical importance is the fact that the goals set by these companies are *based on customers' requirements and expectations* rather than internal company standards. While some similarity may exist between customers' requirements and company standards, we find many instances where service companies are measuring and monitoring internal standards for features that customers do not care about while ignoring other features that customers do care about.

CLOSING GAP 2: SETTING SERVICE-QUALITY GOALS

Effective service-quality goals have several common characteristics. Most important, they are based on customers' requirements. They are also specific. They are accepted by employees and cover important job dimensions. They are measured and reviewed with appropriate feedback. Finally, effective goals are challenging but realistic.[27]

1. *Designed to Meet Customers' Expectations.* American Express, after analyzing customers' complaints, surveys, and other customer data, found that timeliness, accuracy, and responsiveness were the important dimensions of quality to its customers. Management then identified 180 goals for different aspects of these customer-oriented dimensions rather than company-oriented dimensions of service quality.[28] Next, the company determined which performance levels the customers expected (rather than what the company wanted to establish) on each of the contacts customers had with the company.

2. *Specific.* Effective service goals are defined in *specific* ways that enable providers to understand what they are being asked to deliver. At best, these goals are set and measured in specific responses to human or machine performance. Goals should not be vague, as in "answer phones quickly" or "get the customer through the line as fast as possible." Instead, goals should be clear and specific as illustrated by the following quote from an American Airlines executive:

> We have goals and standards for almost every area of the operation, and we check them on a regular basis. We are constantly measuring how long it takes us to answer a reservations call, or process a customer in a ticket line, or get a plane-load of passengers on board the aircraft, or open the door of the airplane once it reaches its destination, or get food on, or get trash off.[29]

The specific measures of these activities form the baseline for performance at American Airlines and the standard on which all ensuing transactions are measured.

3. *Accepted by Employees.* Employees perform to standards consistently only if they understand and accept the goals. Imposing standards on unwilling employees often leads to resistance, resentment, absenteeism, or even turnover. Many companies establish standards for the amount of time it should take (rather than what it does take) for each service job and gradually cut back on the time to reduce labor costs. This practice inevitably leads to increasing tensions among employees. In these situations, managers, financial personnel, and union employees can work together to

determine new standards for the tasks. Through this participation, commitment of the line organization can be obtained and standards are accepted and more accurate.

4. *Important Job Dimensions.* As we saw in chapter 2, perceived service quality is a function of different dimensions. Most service workers cannot deliver to all of these dimensions at the same time. It is absolutely essential that management set priorities for these service workers, giving them clear messages about which aspects of the service job are most critical. One effective way to assure that the important tasks are accomplished by employees is to emphasize these important tasks in the goal-setting process. Most service customers in our research wanted reliability above all else. In the companies we studied, setting standards to do the job right the first time (reliability) would be emphasized above all else.

5. *Measured and Reviewed with Appropriate Feedback* To be effective, goals must be measured and reviewed regularly. Without measurement and feedback, corrections to quality problems will probably not occur. James Robinson of American Express puts it this way: "Employees do what management *inspects*, not what management *expects*."[30]

American Airlines' service goal approach illustrates the effective use of measurement and feedback:

> Reservation phones must be answered within 20 seconds, 85% of flights must take off within five minutes of departure time and land within 15 minutes of arrival time. Cabins must have their proper supply of magazines. Performance summaries drawn up every month tell management how the airline is doing and where the problems lie. The late arrivals may have been caused by disgruntled air controllers which can't be helped. But an outbreak of dirty ashtrays may be traced to a particular clean-up crew. The manager responsible for the crew will hear about it. His pay and promotion depend on meeting standards.[31]

American Express has an elaborate monitoring and tracking system for service quality. The system reflects the impact of any employee or department that interacts with customers. Called the Service Tracking Report, the system measures performance to the goals, such as the time it takes to process new applications, replace lost or stolen cards, or solve merchant problems. Quality assurance personnel regularly take samples of work and measure performance against these standards. The managers meet regularly to review recordings of telephone conversations and discuss ways to improve the handling of calls.[32]

6. *Challenging but Realistic.* A large number of studies on goal setting show that highest performance levels are obtained when goals are challenging but realistic. If goals are not challenging, employees get little reinforcement for mastering them. On the other hand, unrealistically high goals leave an employee feeling dissatisfied with performance and frustrated by not being able to attain the goal.

EMPIRICAL FINDINGS ABOUT GAP 2

We investigated the size of Gap 2 and the impact of the four factors described in this chapter in five major U.S. service companies. As described in chapter 4, we surveyed managers and contact personnel in these service companies, measuring their perceptions of the extent of Gap 2 and the factors likely to influence it. The results of this research are shown in exhibit 5–3 by company (numbered 1–5). On the left side of the charts, bar 1 shows the size of Gap 2 as perceived by managers and bar 2 by contact personnel. The solid sections of these bars indicate the current status of the gap in each of the companies (the higher the number, the smaller the gap). The patterned sections of these bars indicate opportunities for gap closure. For example, managers in company 1 perceive a bigger Gap 2 than those in company 3. The bars to the right show the levels of perceptions of individual factors (management's commitment to service quality, goal setting, task standardization, and perception of feasibility) responsible for Gap 2. As with Gap 2 bars on the left, the solid part of each bar on the right shows the current status on the factor as perceived by managers and the patterned section shows the opportunity for improvement in the factor. In company 1, for example, the smallest gap is in goal setting; it appears that the company has a goal-setting process in place. On the other hand, company 1 has a long way to go in management's commitment to service quality. If the company is serious about quality, management must become more committed, communicate that commitment to employees, and actually set goals focused on service quality.

An interesting pattern of results across companies is that contact personnel's perceptions of the size of Gap 2 are consistently higher (except in one case in which they are the same) than managers' perceptions of Gap 2 in the five companies. Contact personnel appear to have a more optimistic view of the size of the Gap 2 than does management.

The data shown in these charts reveal that different factors are likely to be responsible for Gap 2 in different companies. The size of the gaps

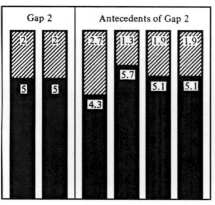

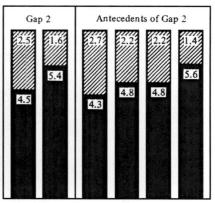

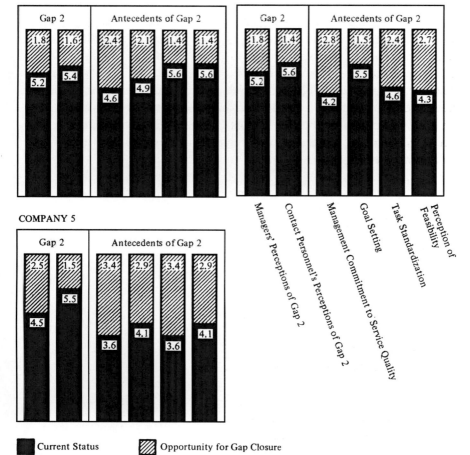

Current Status   Opportunity for Gap Closure

Exhibit 5–3 Gap 2 and Its Antecedents

in the individual factors are different across sample firms, suggesting that Gap 2 may have different drivers in different companies. For this reason, companies need to monitor all factors and determine through this type of analysis which factors are critical in their particular organizations. The factors identified as most critical would be targets for immediate attention for closing Gap 2.

Appendix B contains instructions and questionnaires for performing the type of gap analysis shown in exhibit 5–3.

SUMMARY

This chapter discussed Gap 2, the difference between management's perceptions of customers' expectations and the standards they set to fulfill these expectations. Our research indicates that the major reasons for Gap 2 include (1) inadequate management commitment to service quality; (2) lack of perception of feasibility; (3) inadequate task standardization; and (4) absence of goal setting.

Each of these reasons is discussed and detailed in this chapter, along with strategies to close the gap. To deliver high service quality, managers need the vision and commitment to change the systems of service delivery to meet customers' perceptions. This change often requires new equipment, technology, processes, and integration of executives from many different parts of the firm.

6

◇ ◇ ◇

GAP 3: THE SERVICE PERFORMANCE GAP

W E DEALT IN CHAPTER 4 with management's understanding of customers' expectations and in chapter 5 with the specifications management establishes to deliver to those expectations. In some cases
management does understand customers' expectations and does set appropriate specifications (either informally or formally), and still the service delivered by the organization falls short of what customers expect.
The difference between service specifications and the actual service delivery is the *service-performance gap*: when employees are unable and/or
unwilling to perform the service at the desired level. Unfortunately, this
service-performance gap is common in service businesses.

Organizations offering services that are highly interactive, labor intensive, and performed in multiple locations are especially vulnerable to Gap
3. Opportunities for mistakes and misunderstandings exist when service
providers and customers interact: both customers and providers experience and respond to each other's mannerisms, attitudes, competencies,
moods, and language. Greater variability is also more likely in labor-
intensive services than when machines dominate service delivery. Bank
customers who use human tellers experience far more service variability
than those using automatic teller machines. Finally, when service is produced in a chain of outlets, quality control is complicated because the
organizational layers between senior management and frontline service
providers hinder two way communication and make it more difficult to
assess individual employees' performance.

Service quality suffers when employees are unwilling or unable to
perform a service at the level required. Willingness to perform may be
described as discretionary effort, the difference "between the maximum
amount of effort and care that an individual could bring to his or her job,

and the minimum amount of effort required to avoid being fired or penalized."[1] Employees who begin a new job giving 100 percent discretionary effort may be giving far less within weeks or months. This can happen because they have had to deal with too many long lines, too many unreasonable customers, too many rules and regulations, and too few pats on the back. It can also happen when they observe that few of their associates are giving their jobs their all.

In other cases, service providers may simply not have the ability to perform at specified levels. An organization may offer wage rates insufficient to attract skilled workers, or it may fail to train personnel adequately, or both. In addition, as a result of high turnover, workers may be moved into higher-level positions before they are ready. These factors are typical of many service industries, and all can lead to poor service quality.

Maintaining service quality, then, depends not only on recognizing customers' desires and establishing appropriate standards but also on maintaining a work force of people both willing and able to perform at specified levels.

Our extensive research focusing on the provider's side of our gaps model indicates that seven key conceptual factors contribute to Gap 3, the service-performance gap. These factors, illustrated in exhibit 6–1, include: (1) *role ambiguity*; (2) *role conflict*; (3) *poor employee-job fit*; (4) *poor technology-job fit*; (5) *inappropriate supervisory control systems* leading to an inappropriate evaluation/compensation system; (6) *lack of perceived control* on the part of employees; and (7) *lack of teamwork*. Exhibit 6–2 defines these factors and presents several specific issues about them. In this chapter, we describe the problems stemming from these factors and offer suggestions for dealing with them to close Gap 3. We then discuss empirical findings from our research pertaining to Gap 3 and the organizational factors contributing to it.

GAP 3 PROBLEM: EMPLOYEE ROLE AMBIGUITY

The role attached to any position in an organization represents the set of behaviors and activities to be performed by the person occupying that position.[2] The role is defined through the expectations, demands, and pressures communicated to employees by individuals (e.g., top managers, immediate supervisors, customers) who have a vested interest in how employees perform their jobs. When employees do not possess the information or training necessary to perform their jobs adequately, they

Exhibit 6–1 Key Factors Contributing to GAP 3

experience *role ambiguity*. They are uncertain about what managers or supervisors expect from them and how to satisfy those expectations. They do not have the training or the skills to provide the service necessary to satisfy customers. Further, they do not know how their performance will be evaluated and rewarded.

The status of training in many firms is bleak—too little too late. A customer-service representative in one of our studies commented: "It's really embarrassing—customers know about new products before we do. We're the company. We should know things before the customer does. But the training classes may be scheduled after the product comes out." During a focus group interview in banking, a lending officer expressed a similar complaint: "The bank will put out a product we don't understand—especially loans—and not tell us enough about it, not train us enough to sell it. With XYZ for example, I still have to get out the book [to look up how the loan works] and it takes me a good ten minutes." At this point, another participant in the group chimed in, "I just found out two weeks ago that we had the book." Then another said, "I just found out that we had XYZ!"

Training is essential in eliminating role ambiguity but employees sometimes lack role clarity in firms with good training. Unless training is supported by clear messages about what managers expect, unless em-

Factor and Definition	Specific Illustrative Issues
Role Ambiguity: Extent to which employees are uncertain about what managers or supervisors expect from them and how to satisfy those expectations.	• Does management provide accurate information to employees concerning job instruction, company policy and procedures, and performance assessment? • Do employees understand the products and services offered by the company? • Are employees able to keep up with changes that affect their jobs? • Are employees trained to interact effectively with customers? • How often does management communicate company goals and expectations to employees? • Do employees understand what managers expect from them and how to satisfy those expectations?
Role Conflict: Extent to which employees perceive that they cannot satisfy all the demands of all the individuals (internal and external customers) they must serve.	• Do customers and managers have the same expectations of employees? • How often do customer-contact employees have to depend on other support services employees to provide quality service to customers? • Do employees have more work to do than they have time to do it? • Does the number of demands in employees' jobs make it difficult to effectively serve customers? • Do too many customers want service at the same time? • Do employees cross-sell services to customers in situations where it is inappropriate?
Employee-Job Fit: The match between the skill of employees and their jobs.	• Do employees believe that they are able to perform their jobs well? • Does the company hire people who are qualified to do their jobs? • Does management devote sufficient time and resources to the hiring and selection of employees?
Technology-Job Fit: The appropriateness of the tools and technology that employees use to perform their jobs.	• Are employees given the tools and equipment needed to perform their jobs well? • How often does equipment fail to operate?

Exhibit 6–2 Conceptual Factors Pertaining to GAP 3

Factor and Definition	Specific Illustrative Issues
Supervisory Control Systems: The appropriateness of the evaluation and reward systems in the company.	· Do employees know what aspects of their jobs will be stressed most in performance evaluations? · Are employees evaluated on how well they interact with customers? · Are employees who do the best job serving customers more likely to be rewarded than other employees? · Do employees who make a special effort to serve customers receive increased financial rewards, career advancement, and/or recognition? · Do employees feel appreciated for their contributions?
Perceived Control: Extent to which employees perceive that they can act flexibly rather than by rote in problem situations encountered in providing services.	· Do employees spend time in their jobs trying to resolve problems over which they have little control? · Are employees given the freedom to make individual decisions to satisfy customers' needs? · Are employees encouraged to learn new ways to better serve their customers? · Are employees required to get approval from another department before delivering service to customers?
Teamwork: Extent to which employees and managers pull together for a common goal.	· Do employees and managers contribute to a team effort in servicing customers? · Do support services employees provide good service to customer-contact personnel? · Are employees personally involved and committed to the company? · Do customer-contact employees cooperate more than they compete with other employees in the company? · Are employees encouraged to work together to provide quality service to customers?

Exhibit 6–2 Continued

ployees know which of their behaviors are appropriate and inappropriate, unless feedback on performance is provided often enough to correct problems, Gap 3 can remain wide.

CLOSING GAP 3: PROVIDING ROLE CLARITY

Management can use four key tools to provide role clarity to employees: communication, feedback, confidence, and competence.[3] First, employees need accurate information about their roles in the organization. They need specific and frequent communication from supervisors and managers about what they are expected to do. They also need to know the goals, strategies, objectives, and philosophy of the company and of their own departments. They need current and complete information about the products and services the company offers. And they need to know the company's customers—who they are, what they expect, and which types of problems they encounter in using the service.

Next, employees need to know how well they are performing compared to the standards and expectations that management sets for them. Feedback provides reinforcement when employees perform well and offers the opportunity for correction when they perform poorly. This feedback need not always come directly from management; self-tracking of performance to key standards (such as the percentage of customer complaints handled within the expected time or the percentage of on-time deliveries) can provide the feedback necessary for employees to clearly understand their performance and roles.

Finally, employees need to feel confident and competent in their jobs. Companies can engender confidence in employees by training them in the skills needed to satisfy customers. Training that relates to the specific services offered by the firm help the contact person be and feel capable when dealing with customers. Training in communication skills, especially in listening to customers and understanding what customers expect, gives employees a sense of mastery over the inevitable problems that arise in service encounters. Training programs should be designed to increase employees' level of confidence and competence, which results in greater role clarity and helps close Gap 3.

Technical Training. It seems obvious that employees need training in the technical aspects of the services they provide. Yet many companies fall short of providing the technical knowledge and training necessary. One source of this problem is the proliferation of services in the service line—too many new services, too much added complexity, too short a lead time in introducing the services. Almost all the companies we studied were characterized by extensive additions to their service lines. In the case of the financial service firms, a clear impetus was deregulation. In the case of a repair firm, the impetus was electronics technology and its new product offspring: camcorders, videocassette recorders; home computers; and touch-sensitive, electronically timed washing machines.

To cope with new services, sophisticated customers, and technical complexity, firms need to develop strong training programs for employees. Merck & Company, the top-rated pharmaceutical firm in serving pharmacists and doctors, recognizes the necessity of training salespeople for the technical aspects of their jobs. The company's 11-month extensive program provides training in basic medical subjects (such as anatomy, physiology, and disease), Merck's products, presentation skills, and current topics in medicine. The program includes more than 13 weeks in a classroom, on-the-job training in the field, and medical classes conducted at universities known for the quality of their medical programs.[4]

Goodyear Tire & Rubber Company trains its entire service force to answer any and all questions customers may ask. To equip them for this challenge, the company designed a comprehensive training program that included specifics about the services and functions of the various departments as well as general training in consumer education and customer service. Similarly, Du Pont requires anyone who sells for its chemicals and pigments division to have worked in some other capacity at Du Pont for two years and also to have completed a year's training in business analysis and distribution.[5]

Training in Interpersonal Skills. Dealing with customers can be hard work, particularly when customers are demanding, hurried, dissatisfied, or angry. Unfortunately, demand fluctuations and other uncontrollable factors mean that all service workers at some point encounter disgruntled customers. Firms can and do develop employees to deal with these problems by training in interpersonal skills:

- British Airways is known for its training sessions in coping with the stress of customer contact that comes with intensive customer-service activities. The company put its entire 37,000-person customer-service staff through a training program called Putting People First which helps employees learn how to communicate effectively under pressure.[6] In one workshop exercise, half the participants were blindfolded and taken care of through a dinner meal by the other half. The purpose of this exercise and the training program as a whole was "to help people to ask for the kind of help they need on the one side, and on the other side to experience what it is like to give help that is required rather than the help you want to give."[7]

- At Stew Leonard's dairy store, over half of the 450 employees have gone through the Dale Carnegie program.[8]
- At Einstein Medical Center in Philadelphia, employees attend seminars where they take turns playing patient and learn a set of house rules for patient contact that include: "Make eye contact. Introduce yourself. Call people by name. Explain what you're doing." Einstein also has an ongoing campaign called HOSPITAL-ity to motivate everyone from janitors to doctors to be more courteous. Although doctors resisted initially, they "gradually discovered that they could act a great deal nicer and that patients noticed the difference." The service-quality excellence ratings of the center rose from 43 to 85 percent in three years.[9]
- Schaeffer & Sons Jewelers developed a training program to show employees how to transform complaints into sales. The four basic steps in the complaint handling process the company used were: open lines of communication; ask specific questions to get to the root of the problem; work within company policy to solve the problem; and reaffirm the customer's faith in the company's reputation.[10]

Teaching Employees about Customers. Although conventional wisdom holds that contact employees know customers well, perhaps even better than management knows them, we believe it essential to provide training about customers. One of our research studies (see exhibit 4–4) reveals that in the companies we studied, management perceives customers' expectations more accurately than contact employees perceive them. We speculate that managers in our study had access to research information about customers' needs and wants that they did not share with the contact employees. The more contact personnel know about customers' expectations, perceptions, and problems, the better they can serve them. Training contact personnel about their customers is emphasized in companies known for their service excellence. Milliken, the textiles company lauded for its customer service, includes an internship in manufacturing for all salespeople, and a stand-in-the-customer's-shoes training program. To provide quality service to their customers, salespeople must understand manufacturing operations because so many of Milliken's service products are used in manufacturing.[11]

GAP 3 PROBLEM: ROLE CONFLICT

Employees of service firms often experience *role conflict*, the perception that they cannot satisfy all the demands of all the individuals they must serve.[12] Many times this occurs because too many customers need or want service at the same time. Conflict between the expectations of the company and the expectations of customers also is not unusual in service firms. For example, conflict occurs when an income tax firm expects staff members to process as many customers as possible in a short time (i.e., limits the time with customers) and customers want personal attention from the staff (e.g., to discuss tax avoidance strategies for the future). Role conflict involves a poor fit among different elements of a service provider's job and creates feelings of tension, anxiety, and dissatisfaction.[13]

Role conflict often results when management emphasizes selling over service and expects employees to sell while they serve. Employees frequently feel they are expected to push these services on customers and many are torn between the company's expectations and their desire to serve customers. Employees in one of the banks we studied provide a clear example of role conflict. The bank had decided to introduce more aggressive personal selling at the branch level by emphasizing the sales component of branch employees' responsibilities. Many service providers view the sales and service elements of their jobs as conflicting. A teller observed: "If I am trying to cross-sell when there's a long line, the customers waiting in line give me that look: 'When is that girl going to shut up?' " One customer-service representative said: "You are torn sometimes between giving the customer what he or she wants and bringing money into the bank."

When faced with this conflict, does the employee take the time to cross-sell services to the customer or simply open the requested account and move on to the waiting customer? Complicating the issue is the reality that they may be measured—and rewarded—on the basis of cross-selling achievements.

Cross-selling is not always in conflict with service. When the employees and the customer have adequate time and the customer has interest, providing information about other company offerings may actually be part of quality service delivery. But when managers ask employees to sell in an aggressive manner or in a role (such as a teller) where selling is inappropriate, role conflict is the result.

The service-versus-sales dichotomy is not the only conflict employees experience. There are often simply too many demands on the employee's attention. The following comment is typical: "You are supposed to give your customer undivided attention, but you have already been interrupted seven times by telephone calls. You can't put the telephone caller on hold or send him elsewhere, because once I did that and the caller was a 'shopper' and my [performance] score was lowered."

The managers of service organizations can also inadvertently create role conflict for employees through excessive paperwork or unnecessary internal roadblocks. For example, customer-service personnel are often required to complete forms for the services they sell or the problems they handle. These employees may experience role conflict if other customers are waiting in a line or on the telephone to be served. Which master should be served, the waiting customer or the growing pile of paperwork?

A final source of role conflict is *role overload* which results from excessive contact with too many customers. Employees in service businesses experience a type of emotional overwork that author Arlie Russell Hochschild calls *contact overload* which leads to flat, frozen emotions.[14]

CLOSING GAP 3: ELIMINATING ROLE CONFLICT

Besides having a negative effect on employees' satisfaction and performance in the organization, role conflict can increase absenteeism and turnover.[15] A service organization that recognizes inherent conflicts in the service provider's job goes far in eliminating the distress of role conflict and its resulting distress on the organization.

If the company defines service roles and standards in terms of customers' expectations, role conflict is minimized. Many companies involve employees in the standard-setting process, believing that they are more knowledgeable than anyone else about their jobs. The advantage in this approach is that employees feel responsible for the service-quality changes they help develop, have a clear idea of what is expected of them, and accept change because they see why the new process is better.

Role conflict can be minimized by reinforcing change with other human resource systems. Use of performance measurement systems that focus on the customer in addition to (or rather than) internal efficiency goals is one way to clearly support the service-quality priority. Another is to train employees in priority setting and time management. Still another is compensation tied to delivery of service quality (by measures of customers' satisfaction, loyalty, perceived service quality) instead of, or as well as, other factors.

For employees suffering from role overload, frequent breaks and varied work tasks have been successful in managing the overload. Employees need time to relax mentally to avoid the burnout of contact overload.

GAP 3 PROBLEM: POOR EMPLOYEE-JOB FIT

Our research indicates that service-quality problems often occur because personnel are not well suited to their positions. Because customer-contact jobs tend to be situated at the lower levels of company organization charts (e.g., car rental agents, telephone operators, and repair technicians), personnel holding these jobs are frequently among the least-educated and lowest-paid employees in their companies. As a result, they may lack language, interpersonal, or other skills to serve customers effectively. Many service companies have high turnover among contact employees and are inclined to fill openings quickly, even if they must hire persons having background or skill deficiencies. Managers commonly do not give enough attention or devote sufficient resources to hiring and selection processes.

The overriding sentiment among disgruntled employees in one of our studies was that you get what you pay for, and the firm wasn't paying for much. One manager said, "We draw from the bottom of the barrel because that's the way we compensate." When management does not match employees to jobs through selection processes that identify those with ability or skill to perform the job well, Gap 3 widens.

GAP 3 PROBLEM: POOR TECHNOLOGY-JOB FIT

Provision of high service quality also depends on the appropriateness of the tools or technology employees use to perform the job. Technology and equipment, such as computers and diagnostic equipment, can enhance the service employee's performance. Appropriate and reliable technology must be provided for high-quality service delivery. Equipment inadequacies and failures can seriously interfere with adequate employee performance.

Our exploratory study revealed several instances in which service-quality shortfalls resulted from a lack of technology-job fit and/or employee-job fit. For example, a product-repair executive, in bemoaning the proliferation of new high-technology appliances, indicated problems stemming from a lack of both types of fit: "We may not have all the [technical] specifications needed to train technicians before a new product is marketed [technology-job fit]. Some technicians may never be capable of being trained to service these new 'high-tech' products [employee-job fit]. These products are coming too fast."

CLOSING GAP 3: IMPROVING EMPLOYEE-TECHNOLOGY-JOB FIT

Competing effectively for first-rate service providers makes it easier to compete for customers. Successful service companies rely on careful selection of employees and technology and the fit among the employee, technology, and the job. Federal Express's company philosophy clearly illustrates the importance of human resources: "Hire the best people, give them the best training and compensation you can, and they'll deliver the high-level efficiency and service that translates into profit. People, service, profit—in that order."[16]

Because competing for talent promises to become more intense in the future—an issue we explore in depth in chapter 9—innovative recruitment and retention methods need to be developed.[17]

A number of major service companies are searching for and finding new ways to recruit and retain lower-level service employees. ServiceMaster Company, the successful franchised janitorial service, hires many people who are functionally illiterate. The company's CEO, recognizing the importance of these employees to the business, has adopted an approach that respects them and gains their loyalty. He believes that, "before asking someone to do something you have to help them to be something."[18] The company provides self-development programs to help the employees improve their lives. Another ServiceMaster Company slogan is "to help people grow." When a hospital served by the company decided to hire a deaf person as one of its contacts, ServiceMaster's local manager didn't object. Instead he authorized three of his supervisors to take a course in sign language.[19]

Wegman's, a large, successful grocery chain in Rochester, New York, suffered from the same problems as all employers who pay minimum wage. The company hired what it called the rawest of recruits and was plagued by high turnover among them. The company now has a program that develops these recruits personally and encourages them to stay with the firm. For those who work at Wegman's for at least a year, perform well in their jobs, and seem likely to do well in college or graduate school, the company offers scholarships for half their tuition. "Almost 1,000 of

Wegman's 11,000 full- and part-time employees have made the grade, stayed in school, and at Wegman's."[20]

Compensating employees at a higher-than-market level can also engender loyalty. Somerville Lumber & Supply, the Massachusetts company that retails lumber and other construction materials, pays employees more than other firms in its industry, starting them at an annual salary of about $20,000. The company pays an additional 15 percent of salary into a profit-sharing fund. Employees are entitled to a portion of that money if they stay for more than three years, and get the entire portion if they stay ten years. Many ten-year employees have accrued $100,000 and some longer-term employees are millionaires. Moreover, the profit-sharing plan is supplemented by a pension plan, under which another 10 percent of salary is set aside.[21]

Embassy Suites, Inc., a division of Holiday Corporation, believes that employees who have a chance to grow in their jobs are more likely to be satisfied and loyal to the company. To build growth into low-level positions such as housekeeping, the company offers an opportunity for all employees to cross-train for other positions in the company. Housekeeping personnel can learn how to work the front desk; food service personnel can learn housekeeping. For each new position employees learn, they receive a boost in their hourly pay. As employees develop personally and financially, the company creates a ready source of trained and flexible personnel for peak periods or understaffed times.[22]

Competing effectively for first-rate service providers is essential to success in a service business. Companies that excel in service select and develop employees carefully, choose appropriate technology, and concentrate on the fit among employees, technology, and jobs.

GAP 3 PROBLEM: INAPPROPRIATE SUPERVISORY CONTROL SYSTEMS

In many service organizations, the performance of contact employees is measured by their output (e.g., the number of units produced per hour, the number or amount of sales per week). In these *output control systems*, the performance of individuals is monitored and rewarded not for service-quality delivery but for other company-defined goals.[23] These output measures alone are usually inappropriate or insufficient for measuring employees' performance relating to the provision of quality service. For example, most bank customers want bank tellers to be accurate, fast, and friendly. Banks that measure tellers' performance strictly on output measures, such as end-of-the day balancing of transactions, overlook key aspects of job performance that customers factor into quality-of-service perceptions.

CLOSING GAP 3: MEASURING AND REWARDING SERVICE PERFORMANCE

In service situations where the manner in which service is provided is essential to customers' satisfaction, performance also can be monitored through what are termed *behavioral control systems*. Behavioral control systems consist largely of observations or other reports on the way the employee works or behaves.[24] The use of behavioral control systems is illustrated by an ongoing "tone-of-service" survey with customers who have recently opened accounts at The Friendly National Bank of Oklahoma City.[25] Customers answer questions about the way they are treated by the customer-service representatives opening their accounts. Friendly also monitors customer-service representatives' performance through ongoing shopper research (researchers pretending to be customers) and a cross-sales index. Each month, customer-service representatives receive tone-of-service and shopper scores (behavioral measures) and a cross-sales score (output measure). The use of these behavioral measures encourages employees' performance to be consistent with customers' expectations of quality service.

A vital ingredient for excellent service-quality delivery is recognition of employees' performance. Employees' performance must be continually monitored, compared with service standards, and rewarded when outstanding. A performance-measurement system sensitive to high performance and tied to appropriate rewards can be very motivating, especially when workers know that others will learn how well they are performing. This system also helps management determine the specific effects of policy and personnel changes on operating performance and to weed out individuals who deliver substandard performance.

Performance measurement should extend beyond image tracking, isolated shopping visits, customer-complaint analyses, and other traditional approaches. Although a service performance-measurement system gets employees' attention, only a well-executed reward system keeps it. Workers realize that management is serious about quality when management is willing to pay for it. A good reward system, like a good measurement system, is one that is meaningful, timely, simple, accurate, and fair.

We recommend using a reward system under which employees are expected to meet service-quality standards and are rewarded for outstanding performance. Rewards can take many forms: direct financial rewards (merit salary increases and bonuses), career advancement, and recognition. The most effective system is one that incorporates all three approaches for both individuals and work groups. Singling out high-performing work units can energize peer pressure and lead to better performance.

Compensation and Direct Financial Incentives. The most convincing way to encourage active support for first-line service employees and middle managers is to tie compensation into performance and behaviors that lead to high service quality. At British Airways, middle managers are evaluated by bosses according to a list of 60 statements of behavior that had been identified as the key behavior characteristics necessary in providing quality customer service. Managers receive lump-sum bonuses worth up to 20 percent of their base salary, half determined by what they achieve and half by the behaviors by which they achieve it.[26]

Commitment to quality on the part of employees is also encouraged by profit-sharing programs. For example, at Publix Fruit & Produce, the food retailer, employees own 62 percent of the company's stock and get back 20 percent of the profits, "right down to the bagboys. . . . The result is workers who hustle. Energetic store clerks seem to be everywhere. Happy employees, in turn, lead to happy customers."[27]

Recognition Programs that Work. Not all employee recognition programs have what it takes to be successful: challenging standards, acceptance by employees, neither too few nor too many rewards, and longevity. Federal Express has a tiered recognition program that works. At the first level, the Bravo Zulu award (meaning "well done" in military terms) of up to $100 can be given by anyone in management to any employee providing excellent customer service. A special flag stamp is affixed to the letter accompanying the award.[28] At the next higher level, Federal Express honors a handful of nonmanagement individuals with its Golden Falcon award each month, recognizing efforts that are "above and beyond their customary line of duty." This award includes a gold pin with the gold falcon emblem and ten shares of Federal Express stock.[29]

John Creedon, president and CEO of Metropolitan Life Insurance Company, instituted a highly creative and powerful recognition program in which 1,000 of the company's 36,000 plus service employees are eligible to win quality awards at $1,000 each. As in the previous Federal Express example, the awards were designed to recognize employees who performed uniquely to provide excellent service quality. Employees nominate themselves or are nominated by others by documenting in writing a single-page description of efforts resulting in a high level of customer satisfaction that also enhances Metropolitan Life's reputation for service quality. Creedon personally selects the final awardees after reviewing all the documented entries. The awards program is a strong signal of the value top management places on customer satisfaction and employee creativity in delivering it.[30]

Financial Rewards for Teams. Companies can use team rewards as an incentive. Domino's Pizza uses what it calls its TIPO (Team/Individual/ Performance/Objectives) system to relate the monthly bonus to individual and team performance for a given period. The process begins by developing key satisfaction indicators for each unit and each specific job in quantifiable terms. Next, weights are assigned to the key indicators to emphasize the priority each key indicator has for customers. The expected level of performance is set, and then measured using phone surveys of customers. If the expected level is obtained, the team wins a monthly bonus.[31]

GAP 3 PROBLEM: LACK OF PERCEIVED CONTROL

Employees' reactions to stressful situations depend on whether they feel they can control those situations.[32] *Perceived control* involves the ability to make responses that influence threatening situations and the ability to choose outcomes or goals.[33] We believe that when service employees perceive themselves to be in control of situations they encounter in their jobs, they experience less stress. Lower levels of stress, in turn, lead to higher performance. When employees perceive that they can act flexibly rather than by rote in problem situations encountered in providing services, control increases and performance improves.

When employees do not feel a sense of personal control over the quality of service rendered, they feel helpless and discouraged about their jobs. In one of our studies in banks, for example, branch lenders used to process and approve loans. Then loan processing and credit decisions were transferred to remote operations centers. As a result, loan decisions move more slowly through the system and branch employees are not able to give customers timely information on the status of their applications. One branch lender said, "My number-one priority is working with other units over which I have no control." A branch manager put it this way: "We're offering terrible service now. We used to have control and now we don't. We used to know where everything is and now we don't."

Perceived control can be low when organizational rules, procedures, and culture limit the contact employees' flexibility in serving customers. It can also be low when the authority to achieve specific outcomes with customers lies elsewhere in the organization. Service companies commonly are organized internally in a way that makes providing fast service to customers difficult for service employees. When a contact person must get the approval of other departments in the organization before delivering a service, service quality is jeopardized. Though the contact person may be totally committed to serving the customer, he or she cannot perform well because control over the service is in the hands of an employee in another place in the organization. Finally, perceived control can be a function of the unpredictability of demand, a major problem in many service businesses.

CLOSING GAP 3: EMPOWERING SERVICE EMPLOYEES

Empowering service employees to satisfy customers helps them develop in the job and the company. Larry Wilson of Pecos Training puts it this way: "Help people find their power and use it in important ways. Give them a chance to find their courage . . . leadership is waking people up."[34] Empowered employees are committed employees, ones who serve the company and its customers well. Jim Kuhn, McDonald's corporate vice-president for individuality, says the key to motivating employees is to "Get out of their way. Believe in your folks and most will live up to your expectations."[35]

Empowerment means pushing decision-making power down to the lowest levels of the company. It means granting contact personnel the authority to make important decisions about serving customers. Empowerment also means replacing heavily standardized and mechanistic approaches for dealing with customers with looser structures that allow employees to individualize their skills and methods. Empowerment can create quick problem solutions for customers because permission to execute a transaction to satisfy customers need not be obtained from multiple employees.

Some service firms are legendary for their empowerment of contact people who go out of their way for their customers. A favorite legend at United Parcel Service is the regional manager who took it on himself to untangle a misdirected shipment of Christmas presents by hiring an entire train and diverting two UPS-owned 727s from their flight plans. When top management learned of his actions, it praised and rewarded him.[36]

Part of Federal Express's legendary company culture is its collection of stories of employee empowerment and dedication to customers. From a deliveryman hefting a 300-pound Fedex deposit box on a truck because he didn't have the key to open it, to a tracing agent who put in place the systems to rescue Baby Jessica from the well she had fallen into, Federal Express employees will do most anything the company allows them to do—and it allows, even encourages, them to do a lot. One legend describes a courier who spent Labor Day saving an ill child:

> A Federal Express courier responded to a Labor Day call from the Memphis trace department regarding a supply of matched blood needed by a child scheduled for surgery at Boston's Children's Hospital the next day. The Boston station's beeper was not functioning; the courier who then arrived at the station in person had to scale a barbed wire fence because his key would not open a new lock on the gate, explain the unusual circumstances to the security guard, find and deliver the package.[37]

One of the things that makes empowerment easier is an internal management information system that can provide unusually helpful information. At Walt Disney World, the story is told about a family who visited Epcot Center and neglected to make note of their parking area. Because Disney maintains daily computerized data that tells which parking lots are filled at what time in the day, employees were able to help the family find their car. With this data system, Disney employees located the car in less than 20 minutes using the family's time of arrival at the center. The guests were driven to the designated parking lot and up and down each row until their car was found.[38]

Empowerment is also effective at managerial levels of a company where department or field managers are given the power to make important company decisions to serve customers. At Byerly's, the grocery chain in Minnesota, deli managers are given complete control in their departments to create new products and expand the deli's selling potential.[39] Each Byerly's store is managed semi-independently by a single executive, who tailors the merchandising to neighborhood needs with little overseeing from top management.[40] The result? Satisfied customers who cannot get enough of the company and its products.

Executives often ask how it is possible to standardize service across departments and outlets and yet still provide sufficient perceived control to bring out the best in employees. Reconciling these two conflicting forces is admittedly difficult. One successful way to balance these forces is to require that managers or departments achieve certain essential goals and standards, allowing them to reach the goals in ways they choose. An example of attempting this balance is illustrated by Au Bon Pain, a chain of bakery and deli shops.

> Store managers are hired on the basis of wanting to solve their own problems. The company, in effect, leases the stores to its managers, gives them goals for labor and food costs, but agrees to split the controllable profits on a 50-50 basis. Like company owners, they have to solve their own problems, hire and fire their own people, set their own wage scale, cut their own deals. What they can't do is to compromise on food quality and customer service, which the company regularly monitors through in-store audits and visits by unidentified "mystery" shoppers. Aside from that, they're on their own. The stores have never run better or with less support from headquarters.[41]

GAP 3 PROBLEM: LACK OF TEAMWORK

The value of teamwork—employees and managers pulling together for a common goal—is a recurring theme in all our studies of service quality. The following statements from one of our studies illustrate a situation where bank employees did not feel they were working together well.

LENDING OFFICER: "I worked in the bank 13 years. There is a big difference in when I started and now in terms of how the employees feel about the bank. There used to be so much camaraderie. Now, it's like pulling teeth to get associates to help you."

CUSTOMER-SERVICE REPRESENTATIVE: "We're *not* working as a family and as a group. We may all come together again but it hasn't happened yet."

CUSTOMER-SERVICE REPRESENTATIVE: "Our cashier sits there and smokes cigarettes and drinks coffee. She doesn't help with any of our work. She says it isn't in her job description. She's a deadbeat."

One aspect of teamwork is the extent to which employees view other employees as customers. In many companies, support employees must provide good service to contact people to enable them to serve customers. Some businesses underestimate the importance to service quality of support services. While customer-contact personnel are obvious targets for quality-improvement efforts, the providers of internal support services are also critical. Poor service to customer-contact personnel results in poor service by those personnel.

Another aspect of teamwork involves the extent to which employees feel personally involved and committed to the firm. Strong belief in an organization and in the importance of one's contribution to it can inspire strong discretionary effort by workers; weak belief can have the opposite effect. To some extent, this employee commitment comes from the sense that management cares about them. In many companies, service people feel that individual performance goes unnoticed and unrewarded. One employee commented: "You feel like management doesn't know what you are doing. We need more support and recognition." Another said, "They should give recognition to people who are really performing. So many times you are judged by your immediate supervisor. That person may not like you. I wish other managers, higher up, would know how people are performing."

CLOSING GAP 3: BUILDING TEAMWORK

In organizations where teamwork exists, employees accomplish their goals by allowing group members to participate in decisions and to share in the group's success. Teamwork is the heart of service-quality initiatives—employees need to work together to have service come together for customers. Merrill Lynch has involved more than twenty-five hundred operations personnel in quality teams of 8 to 15 employees plus a supervisor; each team works to improve customer-service.[42] One group in the cashier's department saved Merrill $40,000 per year with a single idea: By daily updating of securities eligibility data from the Depository Trust Company, they could significantly reduce Merrill's reject ratio, saving money and improving customer service.[43]

Employees at all levels at American Express are required to learn the way that all departments work so that each understands the impact of his or her function on customers' perception of service.

We concluded that the customer-service department is only the catcher's mitt. The real problems arise in other departments: data processing, mail room, new accounts, accounts receivable, etc. The fact that customer service has processed a customer order in two days is not helpful if the order stays in the mail room for four days, and another four days in data processing. Similarly, accounts receivable is just concerned about receiving funds. Well, that's fine if customers really owe money. But we had better make sure before they start sending dunning letters.[44]

And at Shell Oil Company, more than 10,000 employees have participated in a quality-improvement training program focusing on working together in customer-supplier relationships. Vic Gigurelli, manager of quality improvement, comments: "Shell's emphasis on the internal customer is paying off. It has already provided a common language that engineers, craftsmen, clerical staff and business managers can all share to get work done."[45]

CLOSING GAP 3: MANAGING EXTERNAL CUSTOMERS

In many service businesses, part of the reason employees have difficulty delivering good service is that customers themselves are not fulfilling their roles in service delivery. When customers of an income tax preparation service do not save the necessary receipts, when customers in a bar become unruly, when customers at McDonald's do not clear their own tables—these and other examples of poor customer performance interfere with employees' abilities to deliver to standards set by management. What can a company do to encourage customers to accept their roles in service provision? David Bowen, an authority on the management of service employees, suggests that companies treat customers as "partial employees" and manage them by adapting many of the techniques discussed in this chapter for managing employees.[46] Answering the following questions may help to improve customers' service delivery.

Role clarity: Do customers understand how they are expected to perform their part of the transaction? Do employees provide clear instructions and feedback?

Ability: Are customers able to perform as expected? Are the right segments of customers being chosen?

Compensation: Are valuable rewards offered to customers for performing as expected? Is the price differential between full- and self-service adequate to induce customers to perform?

According to Bowen, management practices that can improve situations where customers are coproducers include providing customers with realistic service previews, training customers how to perform, providing visible rewards (airline personnel selecting passengers with first-class seats for early boarding over those with coach seats), selecting the participating

COMPANY 1

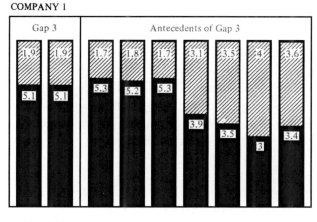

COMPANY 3

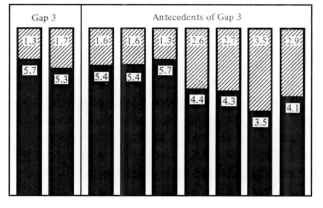

COMPANY 5

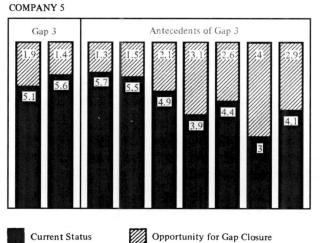

■ Current Status   ▨ Opportunity for Gap Closure

Exhibit 6–3 Gap 3 and Its Antecedents

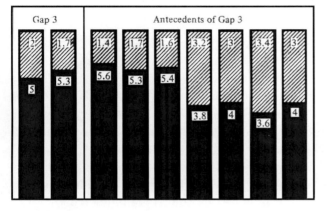

COMPANY 2

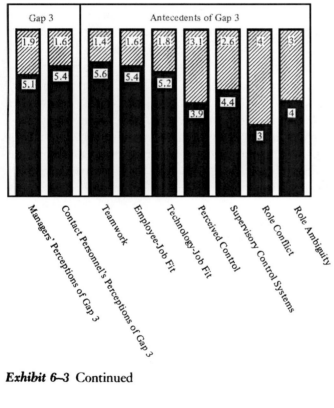

COMPANY 4

Exhibit 6–3 Continued

customer (e.g., those willing to use an automatic teller machine or pump their own gas), and providing customer scripts so that they know what is expected of them.

EMPIRICAL FINDINGS ABOUT GAP 3

We investigated the size of Gap 3 and the impact of the factors described in this chapter in five major U.S. service companies. As described in chapter 4, we measured managers' and contact personnel's perceptions of the extent of Gap 3 and the factors likely to influence it. The results of this research are shown in exhibit 6–3 by company (numbered 1–5). On the left side of the charts, bar 1 shows the size of Gap 3 as perceived by managers and bar 2 by contact personnel. The solid sections of these bars indicate the current status of the gap in each of the companies (the higher the number, the smaller the gap). The patterned sections of these bars indicate the opportunity for gap closure. For example, managers in company 3 perceive a smaller gap than those in any of the other companies. The bars to the right show the levels of individual factors (teamwork, employee-job fit, technology-job fit, perceived control, supervisory control systems, role conflict, and role ambiguity). As with the Gap 3 bars to the left, the solid part of the bar shows the current status on the factor and the patterned section shows the opportunity for improvement along the factor. (Both role conflict and role ambiguity have been reverse scored so that the interpretation of these factors is the same as with other factors.) A striking result is that in all five companies, *role conflict* is the factor with the biggest gap. It appears that in all our sample firms, employees feel that expectations of them are inconsistent or too demanding. Our sample companies have further to go in improving role conflict than in any other factor in Gap 3.

SUMMARY

We dealt in this chapter with the service-performance gap: when employees are unable and/or unwilling to perform the service at the level desired by management. Unwillingness to perform involves reduction in employees' discretionary effort, a result stemming from too many long lines, too many unreasonable customers, too many rules and regulations, and too few pats on the back.

Factors that contribute to the service-performance gap discussed in this chapter include: (1) role ambiguity; (2) role conflict; (3) poor employee-job fit; (4) poor technology-job fit; (5) inappropriate supervisory control systems leading to an inappropriate evaluation/reward system; (6) lack of perceived control on the part of employees; and (7) lack of teamwork. We described the problems stemming from these factors and offered suggestions for dealing with them to close Gap 3. Finally, we discussed empirical findings from our research pertaining to Gap 3 and its antecedents and explored the implications of those findings.

7

◇ ◇ ◇

GAP 4: WHEN PROMISES DO NOT MATCH DELIVERY

WE PROPOSE that the fourth major cause of low service-quality perceptions is the gap between what a firm promises about a service and what it actually delivers. Accurate and appropriate company communication—advertising, personal selling, and public relations that do not overpromise or misrepresent—is essential to delivering services that customers perceive as high in quality. Because company communications about services promise what people do, and because people cannot be controlled the way machines that produce physical goods can be controlled, the potential for overpromising is high.

Appropriate and accurate communication about services is the responsibility of both marketing and operations: marketing must accurately (if compellingly) reflect what happens in actual service encounters; operations, in turn, must deliver what is promised in communications. If advertising, personal selling, or any other external communication sets up unrealistic expectations for customers, actual encounters disappoint them.

As described in chapter 3, our research suggests that Gap 4 can also occur when companies neglect to inform customers of special quality assurance efforts that are not visible to customers. Customers are not always aware of everything done behind the scenes to serve them well. For instance, most hair styling firms have guarantees that ensure customer satisfaction with haircuts, permanents, and color treatments. However, only a few of them actively communicate these guarantees in advertising because they assume customers know about them. The firm that explicitly communicates the guarantee may be selected over others by a customer who is uncertain about the quality of the service. Even though many competitors provide the same guarantees, the firm that communicates it to customers is the one chosen on that attribute. Making customers aware of standards or efforts to improve service when these efforts are not readily apparent to customers can improve service-quality perceptions. Customers who are aware that a firm is taking concrete steps to serve their best interests are likely to perceive a delivered service in a more favorable way.

Discrepancies between service delivery and external communications, in the form of exaggerated promises and/or the absence of information about service delivery aspects intended to serve customers well, can powerfully affect consumers' perceptions of service quality. Our extensive research focusing on the provider's side of our gaps model indicates that two key conceptual factors contribute to Gap 4. These factors, illustrated in exhibit 7–1, are: (1) *inadequate horizontal communication*, particularly among operations, marketing, and human resources, as well as across

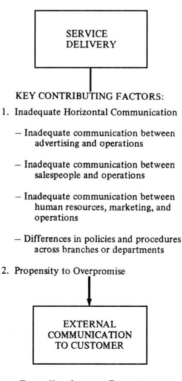

SERVICE DELIVERY

KEY CONTRIBUTING FACTORS:

1. Inadequate Horizontal Communication

   — Inadequate communication between advertising and operations

   — Inadequate communication between salespeople and operations

   — Inadequate communication between human resources, marketing, and operations

   — Differences in policies and procedures across branches or departments

2. Propensity to Overpromise

EXTERNAL COMMUNICATION TO CUSTOMER

Exhibit 7–1 Key Factors Contributing to Gap 4

branches; and (2) *propensity to overpromise* in communications. Exhibit 7–2 defines these factors and presents several specific issues pertaining to them. In this chapter, we describe the problems stemming from these factors and offer suggestions for dealing with them to close Gap 4. We then discuss empirical findings from our research about Gap 4 and the organizational factors contributing to it.

GAP 4 PROBLEM: INADEQUATE HORIZONTAL COMMUNICATIONS

Communications between different functional areas in the firm, such as marketing and operations, are necessary to achieve the common goals of the organization. In situations where communication across functions, or *horizontal communication* channels are not open, perceived service quality is in jeopardy. If, for example, company advertising is developed independent of input from operations, contact personnel may not be able to deliver service that matches the image portrayed in advertising. This lack of communication is illustrated by Holiday Inns, Inc.'s unsuccessful No Surprises advertising campaign. Holiday Inns' advertising agency

Factor and Definition	Specific Illustrative Issues
Horizontal Communication: Extent to which communication occurs both within and between different departments of a company.	• Do customer contact personnel have input in advertising planning and execution? • Are customer contact personnel aware of external communications to customers before they occur? • Does the salesforce interact with customer contact personnel to discuss the level of service that can be delivered to customers? • Are the policies and procedures for serving customers consistent across departments and branches?
Propensity to Overpromise: Extent to which a company's external communications do not accurately reflect what customers receive in the service encounter.	• Is there increasing pressure inside the company to generate new business? • Do competitors overpromise to gain new customers?

Exhibit 7–2 Conceptual Factors Pertaining to Gap 4

found through consumer research that hotel customers wanted greater reliability in lodging and created a television campaign promising no surprises to customers. Top managers accepted the campaign in spite of the skepticism of operations executives who believed that this would be a difficult-to-live-up-to claim. The campaign raised consumers' expectations, gave dissatisfied customers additional reasons to be angry, and had to be discontinued.[1]

Not all organizations advertise, but all need coordination or integration across departments to be able to delivery quality service. All service organizations, for example, need horizontal communication between the sales force and service providers. If customers' expectations are unrealistically raised by salespeople, and if operations personnel cannot deliver on these promises, the size of Gap 4 widens.

Salespeople and operations employees in many companies are often in conflict, each function believing that the other makes work difficult. Operations employees feel that salespeople constantly promise more than they can deliver—usually more quickly than they can deliver—to get or maintain the business. Salespeople, on the other hand, believe that operations employees are unwilling to push hard enough to deliver to customers' expectations. A spirit of misunderstanding and mistrust can develop, enlarging Gap 4. When customers' expectations are raised by salespeople and then not met by service providers, quality perceptions are sacrificed.

Horizontal communication also must occur between the human resources and marketing departments. To deliver excellent customer service, firms must treat their employees as customers.[2] The extent to which the human resource function serves employees through training, motivation, compensation, and recognition has a powerful impact on the quality of service that employees deliver. Breaking down the walls between functions is difficult and time consuming, but high-quality service cannot be delivered without this communication.

CLOSING GAP 4: OPENING CHANNELS OF COMMUNICATION BETWEEN ADVERTISING AND OPERATIONS

When a company creates advertising that depicts the service encounter, it is essential that the advertising accurately reflect what customers experience in actual service encounters. Puffery or exaggeration puts service-quality perceptions at risk, especially when the firm is consistently unable to deliver to the level of service portrayed in advertising. Coordination and communication between advertising and service providers are pivotal in closing Gap 4.

Featuring actual employees doing their jobs or explaining their service in advertising is one way to coordinate advertising portrayals and the reality of the service encounter. Advertising that features actual employees doing their jobs can be very effective in communicating excellence, and the effect is present in both the primary audience (customers) and the secondary audience (employees).[3] An additional benefit is that featured employees become standards for other employees by modeling performance.

In featuring employees, the advertising department must interact directly with service providers. Therefore, the communication and coordination needed to create the advertising helps close the gap between external communications and delivery. Similar benefits can be achieved using other forms of advertising if employees are involved in the advertising process in other ways.

A common complaint of service employees in our studies is that companies run advertisements promising customers certain services or benefits before employees are told about the advertisements and *often before they are told about the services!* Customers come to them asking for the services and they feel uninformed, left out, and helpless.[4] This problem can be avoided by requesting input or opinions from operations employees during the advertising process or by monitoring actual service encounters.

Prior to running advertisements, it is desirable that service providers preview advertising campaigns to prepare them for the service customers will expect them to perform. After that point, the providers must be motivated to carry out the themes of courtesy, responsiveness, and reliability that are presented in advertising. High interdependence exist between advertising and operations, making cooperation and communication between these two functions critical if the promises-delivery gap is to be closed.

When advertising and operations personnel talk to each other, especially when contact personnel provide input to the advertising department about the feasibility of what is being promised in advertising, customers are led to expect what contact personnel can deliver, and Gap 4 can be narrowed.

CLOSING GAP 4: OPENING CHANNELS OF
COMMUNICATIONS BETWEEN SALES AND OPERATIONS

Mechanisms for opening channels of communications between sales and operations employees can take many forms, both formal and informal. Annual planning meetings, retreats, team meetings, or workshops where the departments interact can clarify the issues and allow each department to understand the goals, capabilities, and constraints of the other. A computer company we have worked with planned a "gap workshop" where employees from all functions of a service division met for two days to outline the four gaps in the division and to jointly make plans to close them.

Involving the operations staff in face-to-face meetings with external customers is a strategy that allows operations to more readily understand the salesperson's role and the needs and desires of customers. Rather than filtering customers' needs through the sales force, operations employees can witness firsthand the pressures and demands of customers. A frequent and desirable result is better service to the internal customer (the salesperson) from the operations staff as they become aware of their own roles in satisfying both external and internal customers.

CLOSING GAP 4: OPENING CHANNELS OF
COMMUNICATION BETWEEN HUMAN RESOURCES,
MARKETING, AND OPERATIONS

Because employees are internal customers of the human resource department, the service they receive strongly affects the way they serve external customers. Incentives, training, motivation, and selection must be aligned with service-quality objectives in the company if these internal customers are to deliver high-quality service to external customers.

One effective strategy for opening these channels is a staff position that formally links human resources and operations. The individual who fills this job, often called a service excellence manager, is responsible for developing programs and processes to motivate and facilitate the quality spirit in employees through techniques that include employee recognition and service goals of the company. Karen Caswell, service excellence manager at Citicorp/Citibank, has the full-time job of infusing the service-quality spirit in employees through techniques that include employee recognition and appreciation programs, acknowledgment of new service ideas, and employee newsletters. She views employees as her internal customers and bridges the human resources-marketing gap by educating, motivating, and advertising to employees in the same way that the marketing department communicates with external customers.

GAP 4 PROBLEM: DIFFERENCES IN POLICIES AND PROCEDURES ACROSS BRANCHES OR DEPARTMENTS

Another form of coordination central to providing service quality is consistency in policies and procedures across departments and branches. If a service organization operates many outlets under the same name, whether franchised or company-owned, customers expect similar performance across those outlets. If managers of individual branches or outlets have significant autonomy in procedures and policies, customers may not receive the same level of service quality across the branches. In this case, what they expect and receive from one branch may be different from what is delivered in other branches. Under these circumstances, the size of Gap 4 can be large.

A question frequently asked by companies is, "How much standardization can we achieve across branches without taking away the autonomy and perceived control of managers?" At issue is the need to assure consistency across outlets (so that expectations set by one outlet do not interfere with perceptions of service at another outlet) while allowing the managers autonomy to serve customers in their own ways. If one Command Performance hair styling salon provides hors d'oeuvres and wine for its customers—a touch that can make customers feel special—will customers expect hors d'oeuvres and wine at every Command Performance location and be disappointed if they do not receive the special service? If one McDonald's offers a contest or sweepstakes, won't customers expect it at every McDonald's?

Lack of consistency across outlets explains a large part of the financial and operational difficulties experienced by Jiffy Lube International, Inc., the Baltimore-based franchisor of quick-lube auto centers. Despite the tremendous demand for this new service, the brilliance of the service idea (a quick, efficient, and inexpensive lube job for which customers do not need an appointment), and herculean efforts to ensure similarity of the physical aspects of the service, service-quality perceptions of the firm are low. To respond to heavy demand and to penetrate the market quickly, the company grew from 400 outlets in 1987 to over 1,000 in 1989. Practices to deliver similar service were encouraged—but not required—by the franchisor and the unfortunate result was noticeably uneven service. In the geographic area of one of the authors, for example, three Jiffy Lube franchises produce very diverse service. One site offers outstanding personal service: the service manager consults with the customers several times during service, shows the customer samples of the fluids to be used, asks about problems, and answers questions directly and politely. At the second outlet, the service manager speaks to customers only on arrival and when they settle their bills. In this outlet, each customer must wait in the shop until service is provided because the manager does not want cars that have already been serviced in the parking lot. In contrast, customers in the third outlet may leave their cars for at least an hour, allowing them to run errands or attend to other business in the nearby shopping center. This inconsistency of service, even within the same geographic region, has led to poor word of mouth and customer disappointment with Jiffy Lube and resulted in complaints and class-action suits that severely damage the firm's image.[5]

CLOSING GAP 4: PROVIDING CONSISTENT SERVICE ACROSS BRANCHES OR OUTLETS

If customers are to receive consistent service across branches or field units of a firm, a company must develop a mechanism for ensuring uniformity. In some successful companies, such as the Marriott Corporation, that mechanism is a set of standardized procedures fundamental to the business. Every functional area in Marriott hotels operates under standard operating procedure manuals where all processes and services are carefully documented. Housekeepers, for example, must perform 64 required steps in cleaning a room. These specific guidelines result in uniformly clean rooms anywhere in the Marriott chain. Marriott also allows flexibility and individuality in providing service: Employees are trained to follow these procedures *except when better service can be delivered by the employee* doing something above and beyond the standard to satisfy customers. Because Marriott wants to guarantee this consistently high service, the firm does not franchise its hotel operations but syndicates them instead to investor groups with Marriott retaining 70-year management contracts.

Andersen Consulting, a division of Arthur Andersen & Company and the largest consulting firm in the world, uses a corporate philosophy called the one-firm concept and a strong training program to develop consistency across its multiple locations. The one-firm concept means that all the separate offices operate as a whole—every employee works for Andersen Consulting first and their own office second. Among the ways that the one-firm concept is executed is through central training in sub-urban Chicago. Every professional employee from all over the world is trained in the same way at the same center. Cross-training of personnel, company communications, and the centralized training lead to such sim-ilarity of performance that some employees jokingly call themselves "Arthur Androids." Whatever difficulties experienced by employees us-ing this philosophy, Andersen Consulting enjoys the best reputation for consistent service among the big-eight firms.

A firm may also choose other ways to obtain consistency, perhaps by setting standards or goals for service-quality outcomes that are visible to customers, but allowing the outlets to use their own process to achieve these goals.

GAP 4 PROBLEM: PROPENSITY TO OVERPROMISE

Because of increasing deregulation and intensifying competition in the services sector, many service firms feel more pressure than ever before to acquire new business and to meet or beat competition. To accomplish these ends, service firms often overpromise in selling, advertising, and other company communications. The greater the extent to which a ser-vice firm feels pressured to generate new customers, and perceives that the industry norm is to overpromise ("everyone else in our industry overpromises"), the greater is the firm's propensity to overpromise.

If advertising shows a smiling young lady at the counter in a McDon-ald's commercial, customers expect that—at least most of the time—there will be a smiling young lady in the local McDonald's. If advertising claims that a customer's wake-up call will *always* be on time at a Ramada Inn, customers expect no mistakes. Raising expectations to unrealistic levels may lead to more initial business, but invariably fosters customers' disappointment and discourages repeat business.[6] The propensity to overpromise generates external company communications that do not accurately reflect what customers receive in actual service encounters.

CLOSING GAP 4: DEVELOPING APPROPRIATE
AND EFFECTIVE COMMUNICATIONS
ABOUT SERVICE QUALITY

To be appropriate and effective, communications about service quality must (1) deal with the quality dimensions and features that are most important to customers; (2) accurately reflect what customers actually receive in the service encounter; and (3) help customers understand their roles in performing the service.

EMPHASIZE PRIMARY QUALITY DETERMINANTS

Communicating service quality begins with an understanding of the aspects of service quality that are most important to customers. Isolating quality dimensions most important to customers provides a focus for advertising efforts. Emphasizing the most important dimension or dimensions of service quality results in more effective communications than those focusing on other dimensions.

As we discussed in chapter 2, our research with SERVQUAL has provided surprisingly consistent rankings of the dimensions across service industries.[7] In virtually all the empirical work accomplished thus far, *reliability* stands above all others in importance, regardless of the specific service or industry studied. Customers' expectations of service providers are highest for reliability, and customers rank reliability as the most important of the five dimensions.

If reliability is central to service customers, why don't all companies focus on reliability in advertising? Who do many companies focus instead on other service dimensions such as empathy and tangibles? Our discussions with executives on this subject provides an explanation: On learning that bank customers ranked reliability as the pivotal quality dimension, a banking executive commented: "We're reliable, our competitors are reliable—why focus on something that everyone has?" What this executive perceived about bank reliability may be accurate in an objective sense, but our findings strongly indicate that customers' perceptions do not match managers' perceptions of reliability. In an era of bank closings, failed savings and loan institutions, and increasingly complicated computer technology, many customers doubt the reliability of banks. Executives often *misperceive* that customers of banks—and many other services as well—believe that reliability in their services exists. Customers clearly told us otherwise.

We believe it is essential to obtain perceptions of reliability from the customer before choosing dimensions that are less important than reliability for company advertising. SERVQUAL and related questions described in the appendixes provide a means to investigate these perceptions in individual firms and industries.

MANAGING CUSTOMERS' EXPECTATIONS

A major premise of our research has been that consumers' perceptions of service quality can be influenced either by raising consumers' perceptions or by lowering expectations. Managing customers' expectations, especially those created by the company itself through external communications and price, is an essential part of a strategy to attain perceived quality service.

The expectations customers bring to the service affect their evaluations of its quality: the higher the expectation, the higher the delivered service must be to be perceived as high quality. Therefore, *promising reliability in advertising is only appropriate when reliability is actually delivered.* Promising no surprises at a hotel, as Holiday Inns did, is disastrous if many surprises actually happen in the delivery process. As discussed earlier in this chapter, it is absolutely essential for the marketing or sales department to understand the actual levels of service delivery (e.g., percentage of times the service is provided correctly, percentage and number of problems that arise) before making promises about reliability.

Expectations are the standards or reference points against which a firm's performance is judged. We believe that Gap 4 can be closed by managing customers' expectations—letting customers know what is and is not possible and the reasons why. To manage these expectations, companies must first understand the factors that influence expectations.

"Uncontrollable" Sources of Expectations. As we discussed in chapter 2, our research suggests that word-of-mouth communication, customers' experience with the service, and customers' needs are key factors influencing consumers' expectations. These factors are rarely controllable by the firm; however, an in-depth understanding of these sources and their effects on expectations may lead to strategies that improve perceptions of service.

We are currently investigating the sources of expectations that customers have about service to understand more fully the role that experience plays in the formation of expectations. From our previous work, we have reason to believe that experience with a particular service provider, experience with competitive service providers, and experience with providers of other types of services all influence consumers' expectations. While the first two experiences are readily understood, the third is not so clear. We have found some evidence, for example, that customers' experience with telephone service affects expectations of service from all cable-television companies. Cable-television companies frequently provide service that is perceived by customers to be low in quality, largely because they were comparing the service to that of other service organizations—particularly telephone companies—that are considerably more reliable. This cross-service comparison is intriguing and may account for the unrealistic expectations customers bring with them into many new service encounters.

Firms wanting to investigate these issues may be able to examine research that currently exists in the company about customers' expectations. If research on expectations has yet to be conducted, an approach similar to the one we are using in our own expectations research may be useful. In each of the industries sponsoring our study, we are conducting focus-group interviews with current customers of the type of service the firm provides. An equal number of focus-group interviews involve experienced and inexperienced users of the service because we expect that the sources and levels of expectations will vary in important ways in these two groups. Each focus-group interview covers such topics as sources of customers' expectations of the service, the impact of uncontrollable variables such as word-of-mouth communication and competitors' offerings, as well as company-controlled factors such as those we discuss in the following section.

Controllable Sources of Customers' Expectations. Controllable factors such as company advertising, price, personal selling, and the tangibles associated with the service are likely to be critical in determining the expectations that customers hold for a service.

One of the most frequent questions we are asked on this topic is: "How can we lower expectations without losing business to a competitor who is inflating promises?" This question is particularly difficult when the industry as a whole is suffering from a poor image. Airlines were faced with difficult service delivery problems when the industry was deregulated: overcrowded airports, intense price and route competition, and scheduling problems led to poor service and declining customer perceptions. Airlines knew that reliability—getting to the destination on time safely— was the most important dimension of airline service, but also realized that this was never more difficult to deliver than during the intensely confusing and competitive postderegulation era. Developing an advertising campaign that did not overpromise but engendered awareness and positive perceptions toward a firm was a major challenge. American Airlines ran an advertisement with the headline "Why Does It Seem Like Every Airline Flight Is Late?" that identified with customers' frustrations and explained the key uncontrollable industry reasons for the problems. At the same time, the airline described efforts it was taking to improve the situation. American was comfortable with such claims because it had already documented that its on-time service was better than any of its competitors. Because American's reliability was the highest in the industry, the advertisement was believable and did not stimulate unrealistic expectations. Soon after, American was awarded top billing in service performance by a frequent flyer survey in North America. Later advertisements in the campaign made explicit reliability claims about American's service.

Another way to manage expectations is to describe the service delivery process and provide the customer a choice of quicker, lower-quality provision versus slower, higher-quality provision. In advertising or consulting, for example, speed is often essential but interferes with performance. If customers understand this tradeoff, and are asked to make a choice, they may be more satisfied with their choice because service expectations for each option are realistic.

In both these strategies, marketing reflects a full and accurate understanding of the operations function—how long it takes to accomplish a project, how successfully the company delivers, how often mistakes occur. This communication bridge between marketing and operations, as emphasized earlier in this chapter, is essential in managing expectations.

Price as an Indicator of Service Quality. We believe that price sets expectations for the quality of service, particularly when other cues to quality are not available. When customers lack information about the quality of a service (i.e., when service outcomes are difficult to judge in advance of purchase), they often use price as a surrogate for quality.[8] Because customers depend on price as a cue to quality and because price sets expectations of quality, service prices should be determined carefully. In addition to covering costs or matching competitors, prices must be chosen accurately to convey the appropriate quality signals. Pricing too low can lead to inaccurate inferences about the quality of the service. Pricing too high can set expectations that may be difficult to match in service delivery.

THE CUSTOMER'S ROLE IN SERVICE DELIVERY

Sometimes service problems and failures are caused by customers. Business customers of the postal service frequently put wrong or outdated addresses and zip codes on envelopes. Patients neglect to tell their doctors about unhealthy habits that lead to their medical problems. Restaurant customers are rowdy and interfere with the experience of other diners, and airline customers are irritable and let off steam by yelling at flight attendants. When customers do not accept their responsibilities and roles in service transactions, problems can occur. In many of these situations, communications can be used to encourage customers to be better customers.

New York State Electric and Gas Corporation (NYSEG) has developed many novel ways to help customers be better customers. The company created the *Senior Sun*, a large-type newspaper for senior citizens, to help them make wise and cost-efficient energy decisions. Representatives of the company speak regularly to senior groups about electric and gas safety and efficient energy use.[9] NYSEG also established an education advisory panel through which it offers aids and classroom materials for teachers to increase their understanding of energy issues and their ability to communicate these issues to students.[10]

EMPIRICAL FINDINGS ABOUT GAP 4

We investigated the size of Gap 4 and the impact of the two factors described in this chapter in five major U.S. service companies. As described in chapter 4, we measured managers' and contact personnel's perceptions of the extent of Gap 4 and the factors likely to influence it in service companies. The results of this research are shown in exhibit 7–3 by company (numbered 1–5). On the left side of the charts, bar 1 shows the size of the gap as perceived by managers and bar 2 by contact personnel. The solid sections of these bars indicate the current status of the gap in each of the companies. An interesting pattern that emerges in these charts is that contact personnel tended to perceive the current status of Gap 4 in their companies to be higher than managers' perceptions. In all but company 1, where manager and contact personnel scores are equal, contact people scored higher on the current status of the gap. This indicates that contact personnel in four of the companies have a more optimistic view of the size of the gap than do managers. The patterned sections of these bars indicate the opportunity for Gap 4 closure in each of the companies. Consistent with the observation just discussed, managers perceive that their companies have further to go in closing Gap 4 than contact personnel believe they do.

The bars to the right of the chart show the levels of individual factors of horizontal communication and propensity to overpromise in the five companies. The solid portion of the bar shows the current status on each factor and the patterned section shows the opportunity for gap closure. In company 1, the scores on both factors show large opportunities for gap closure, indicating that the company needs horizontal communication

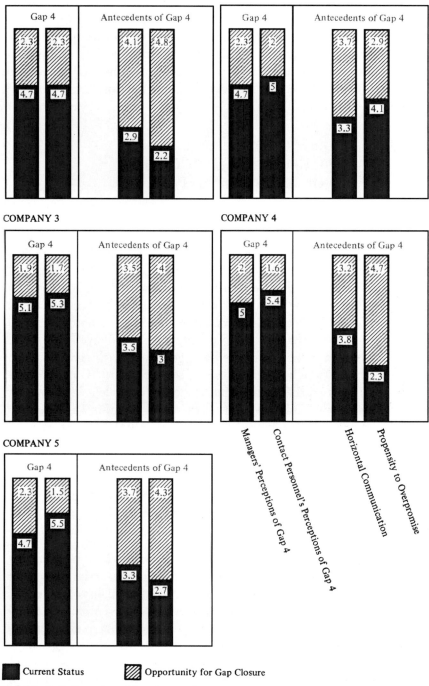

Exhibit 7-3 Gap 4 and Its Antecedents

and that the propensity to overpromise is high. With the exception of company 2, the scores on propensity to overpromise show wide opportunities for gap closure, indicating that overpromising is very high in the industries in which they compete. This pressure to overpromise is likely to inflate customers' expectations and consequently lead to diminished service-quality perceptions. These companies would be well advised to manage customers' expectations in ways suggested in this chapter to close Gap 4.

PUTTING IT ALL TOGETHER: THE EXTENDED GAPS MODEL

The factors we describe in chapters 4 through 7 are germane to an understanding of service-quality shortfalls (i.e., Gaps 1 through 4) and in taking corrective action to ensure the delivery of high-quality service. Exhibit 7–4 is an extended model of service quality, showing the various organizational factors and their relationships to the service-quality gaps. As described in chapter 3, we tested this model by collecting data on the factors and the gaps in five major U.S. service companies. The empirical findings discussed throughout chapters 4–7 came from that extensive field study.

In this extended model, as in the basic gaps model, the gap between customers' expectations and perceptions of service quality (Gap 5) results from the four gaps on the organization's side of the model. As shown on the far right side of exhibit 7–4, customers have expectations and perceptions of Gap 5 on each of the five dimensions. Each of the four organizational gaps (Gaps 1 through 4) in turn is caused by the factors associated with that gap; these are itemized in the left column of the exhibit.

We developed the extended gaps model as a framework for understanding and researching service quality in organizations. The use of this model for research can help a company answer critical questions about service quality such as the following:

1. *Which of the four service-quality gaps is (are) most critical in explaining service-quality variation?* Is one or more of the four managerial gaps more critical than the others in affecting perceived service quality? Can creating one favorable gap (e.g., making Gap 4 favorable by employing effective external communications to create realistic consumer expectations and to enhance consumers' perceptions) offset service-quality problems stemming from other gaps? To answer these questions, firms can use SERVQUAL to capture customers' perceptions and the measures of

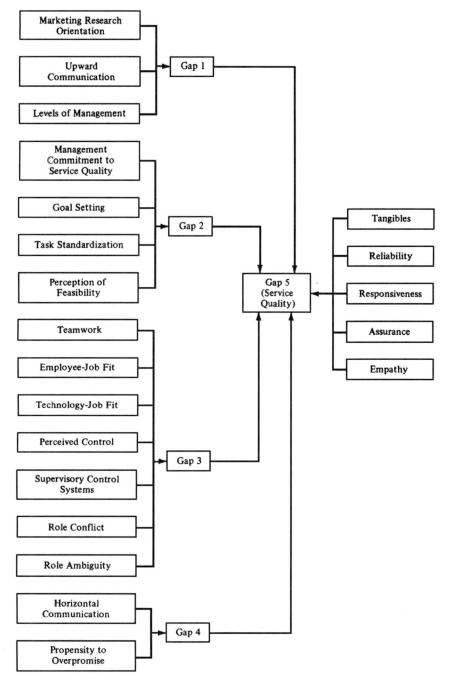

Exhibit 7-4 The Extended Gaps Model of Service Quality

Gaps 1 through 4 (described in chapter 3 and the appendixes) for employees' and managers' perceptions. Intuitively, it would seem that the first three gaps must be closed in order: customers' expectations must be understood before managers can set appropriate standards (Gap 2) and employees must be trained, motivated, compensated, and informed to close Gap 3. A logical progression, then, in closing the gaps is to try to close Gaps 1 through 3 sequentially. Gap 4, however, can be closed before working on the others by managing customers' expectations—bringing expectations in line with actual delivery by lowering expectations rather than improving service delivery.

2. What are the main organizational factors responsible for the size of each of the four service-quality gaps? A key managerial question involves the relative importance of the specific factors in delivering high-quality service to customers. If a company can implement only a few of the many organizational factors, which ones should be undertaken? To answer this question, we created measures of the organizational factors (e.g., amount of marketing research orientation, extent of teamwork, etc.) and related them to the measures of the four gaps. The results are shown in exhibit 7–5. The charts in this exhibit show Xs on the factors that were statistically significant in each of the five companies.

One conclusion that emerged from our empirical research is that there are multiple drivers of Gap 2. In the five firms, different combinations of factors emerged as significant. Especially important constructs were task standardization, goal setting, and management's commitment to service quality. This result indicates that companies can close Gap 2 in a variety of ways and suggests that there are no hard and fast rules appropriate to all companies.

As shown in the Gap 3 chart, the most important drivers of Gap 3 included teamwork, employee-job fit, perceived control, and role conflict. These four factors were significantly related to Gap 3 in at least two of the five sample firms. Teamwork is significant in four of the five companies, suggesting strongly that teamwork is critical in closing the gap between standards and delivery.

The most important driver of Gap 4 is insufficient horizontal communication, significant in four of the five companies. Inconsistent service policies among different service delivery units and limited interaction between contact personnel and operations personnel are key.

The questionnaires that we developed to measure the four gaps and 16 factors are in the appendixes along with instructions on methodology for implementing gap research in your company.

Gap 2

Factors	Company 1	Company 2	Company 3	Company 4	Company 5
Management Commitment	X				X
Goal Setting			X	X	
Task Standardization	X	X			
Perception of Feasibility			X		

Gap 3

Factors	Company 1	Company 2	Company 3	Company 4	Company 5
Teamwork	X	X		X	X
Employee-Job Fit	X		X	X	
Technology-Job Fit		X			
Perceived Control			X		X
Supervisory Control Systems					
Role Conflict		X		X	
Role Ambiguity	X				

Gap 4

Factors	Company 1	Company 2	Company 3	Company 4	Company 5
Horizontal Communication	X	X	X	X	
Propensity to Overpromise				X	

Exhibit 7–5 Key Drivers of the Gaps: Factors that Are Statistically Significant

SUMMARY

Discrepancies between service delivery and external communications have a strong impact on customers' perceptions of service quality. In this chapter, we discussed the factors affecting the size of Gap 4, the gap between promises and delivery. These factors, illustrated in exhibit 7–1, included: (1) inadequate horizontal communication among operations, marketing, and human resources, as well as across branches; and (2) propensity to overpromise in communications. We defined these factors, described the problems they create in organizations, and offered suggestions for dealing with them to close Gap 4. Finally, we presented empirical findings from our research about Gap 4 and introduced the extended gaps model that integrates all of our research on service quality.

8

◇ ◇ ◇

GETTING STARTED ON THE SERVICE-QUALITY JOURNEY

In a *WALL STREET JOURNAL* ARTICLE, "Service with a Smile? Not by a Mile," Jim Mitchell wrote: "The message of the commercials is 'We want you!' The message of the service is 'We want you unless we have to be creative or courteous or better than barely adequate. In that case, get lost.' " Mitchell's article appeared in 1984. Unfortunately, in the early 1990's, Mitchell's comment is still pertinent.

Clearly, many companies are still struggling to get out of first gear on the service-quality journey. The case for improving service is strong, yet outstanding service quality is more the exception than the rule.

The central question in many organizations is: How do we get started on service improvement? How do we move beyond the sterile hype, the start-stop program mentality, the organizational naysayers and doubters, and the constant pressure for short-term earnings growth? In this chapter we address the question of getting started in service improvement, of actually reshaping an organization's culture and competence. Our focus in the last four chapters has been on the ongoing efforts necessary to close service-quality gaps. In this chapter we shift our attention to *starting* the gap management process, to turning on the engine, backing out of the driveway, pointing the car in the right direction and embarking on the journey. We turn first to an analysis of why getting started is so problematic, and then suggest a series of guidelines for moving forward.

THE SERVICE STRUGGLE

The reason so many organizations are struggling with the challenge of improving service is insufficient leadership. It is a simple but important point. The root cause of deficient service quality is not inadequate structures, systems, or research. The root cause of deficient service is people in organizations with leadership responsibilities who, for whatever reason, do not put these necessaries in place.

Organizations are thwarted in improving service because senior managers, middle managers, and first-line service providers lack the will, knowledge, and/or skills to do their parts to move the organization forward. In service organizations everyone is responsible for quality. Some employees provide internal services in that their customers are inside the organization. Others primarily serve customers outside the organization. Still others serve both internal and external customers.

Each of these employees fits into one of the four "willingness/ability-to-serve" cells at any point in time, as shown in exhibit 8-1. A given employee may be both willing and able to perform excellent service (cell one), willing but unable (cell two), unwilling but able (cell three), or unwilling and unable (cell four). For an organization to "get off the dime" in service and make meaningful strides, it must find ways to move more people into cell one. Occupancy of the other cells at any level—senior or middle management or first-line workers—can foul up the machinery for moving forward. To get started in the gap management process we must think of moving three levels of employees from various states of deficiency to a state of effectiveness, so that they can start to close the gaps that they helped to create.

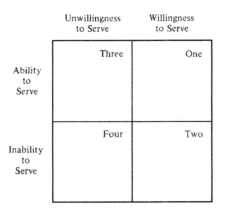

Exhibit 8-1 Willingness/Ability to Serve Matrix

Top Management

It is unusual to think of senior executives as service providers, except in those instances in which they have contact with external customers. As we stressed in earlier chapters, however, senior management must perform a crucial internal service role, the role of service leadership. Only senior management has the position and clout to build an organization's value system on the pillars of satisfying customers, freedom of action, creative problem solving, and respect for employees—essential components of a service-minded culture.[1] Only senior management can build the cultural foundation for quality service in the organization.

To the extent that top management does not conceive and communicate a strong service vision for the firm, does not insist on high standards of internal and external service, does not deal effectively with the naysayers and political game players, does not give service workers the tools they need to do their jobs well, does not recognize and reward exemplary service performers—to the extent that top management does not do these things, they inadequately serve the rest of the organization. It is a simple but powerful truism: top management must provide a strong internal service to unleash a company's true capacity for service excellence.

So what is the problem? Why aren't more top executives like the service leaders we described in chapter 1? For many, the answer is poor understanding and/or skills germane to service leadership, that is, an ability-to-serve problem. It is our experience that some senior executives do not understand the dynamics of service quality well enough to know what to do. This leads to efforts destined for failure, for example, initiating quick-fix programs such as a one-day "smile" training course, delegating primary responsibility for quality improvement to a staff department, or focusing attention strictly on contact personnel and ignoring the critical relationship between internal and external service providers.

Other top executives may know what to do but still may not be able to do it. They may lack the self-confidence to truly lead other people, they may be poor communicators, unable to express a service vision, or they may not have the sensitivity to really understand what others in the organization are saying and feeling.

And for still other senior executives, the key deficiency is one of will, that is, a willingness-to-serve problem. They lack the obsession, the spirit, the commitment to lead the development of a service culture. Service quality is simply not a priority.

- "Average service is good enough."
- "Financial deals drive profits; service issues are just so much mush."
- "Customers won't pay for service, so go for price."
- "American workers are lazy, the work ethic is dead, and mediocre service is inevitable."

These are just a few of the sentiments we hear from top managers—either literally or when we "listen" with our eyes. Consider the sobering words of marketing researcher Mimi Lieber:

> underneath all of the lists, rules, manuals and consumer insight is a core problem we need to address: that our spirit at the top has to change and our attitude toward front-line service be improved. Service is a spiritual and cultural issue. . . . Few on top have been frontline. American managers are still short-term, bottom-line focused. They got where they are generally without concern for spiritual values. They want competitive volume levels *today*, are often more motivated by how to look to the next job in the next company than what *this* company will be in ten years' time. Devoting energy and heart to internal morale, creating the esprit de corps, listening to each other is still considered a job for "personnel."[2]

The task of significantly improving service in large, complex organizations with hundreds or thousands of employees can appear awesome and overwhelming. In addition, improving service generally involves spending money before making money. Without a strong will at the top of the organization, without what Mimi Lieber calls "heart," the service-quality journey will be problematic at best, fruitless at worst.

Middle Managers

One critical group that is often overlooked or given short shrift in the service-quality journey is middle managers—that eclectic body of department heads, supervisors, and others who often serve external customers but who provide internal service as well. The best way to recognize middle-managers' importance in any quest to improve service is simply to reflect on the fact that everyone in the organization works for middle managers, except top managers.

Middle managers are appropriately labeled in one sense, inappropriately labeled in the other. The term *middle* is certainly appropriate. Middle managers are right smack in the middle—of everything. Top management works through middle managers; first-line service providers work for middle managers. Middle managers represent the linkage between the top and bottom of the organizational structure. They can be a conduit for progress or a black hole into which promising ideas mysteriously disappear, for suffocation and burial.

The term *manager*, on the other hand, is less satisfactory. For an organization to truly pursue service excellence, it needs people in the middle who go beyond managing and lead; it needs people in the middle who reinforce the service vision, build a culture of achievement and teamwork in the immediate work unit, and act as role models that show the way and remove service obstacles from the path of subordinates.

Excellent service is not only a function of inspired leadership at the top of organizations; it is also a function of inspired leadership in the middle of organizations. Without question, the quality of leadership service provided by people in the middle of the organization influences directly the quality of service provided by people lower in the organization.

Where the rub comes in is that middle managers in many firms are often ill equipped to be effective service leaders. They may have been promoted to management positions because of their success in technical or sales roles; their leadership qualities and service philosophy may not have been considered at all. And once in these management positions, they may not be held accountable for their willingness or ability to coach, communicate, or model a service ethic.

In many organizations managing is defined as "getting things done through people"; how managers accomplish this task is of little concern. But as our research summarized in this book so clearly shows, the how of management is crucial to improving service; how superiors relate to subordinates can be the difference between awful service and excellent service.

Just how important are middle managers in the service-quality journey? Here is what one prominent bank marketing executive has to say:

> The weakest link in banks, which is an undermining factor of service quality, is middle management. That's where it falls apart. This comes from high turnover at this level, lack of commitment, lack of understanding "the big picture," lack of motivation, and lack of senior management communications. If service quality is ultimately provided by lower levels—tellers, proof operators, transit clerks, loan processors, and the like—then managers of these people are the enforcing link, as well as the promoting link.[3]

And just how tough can it be to transform middle managers from service stranglers to service champions? Here is what Corning Glass Works CEO James Houghton had to say when an interviewer asked him about the resistance he experienced while starting a total quality process at Corning:

> The hardest people to reach are middle managers, and specifically first-line supervisors, because it means a very significant change. Instead of saying, "Do this, do that," first-line supervisors are now being asked to be coaches, to be part of a team, and to listen to their employees on how things could be done better. That takes away some of their management prerogative, which is very hard to deal with. It's very hard for someone who's been doing things the same way for 30 years to be told, "You're still the boss, but you're a different boss."[4]

Middle managers are clearly more central to the twin questions of what causes service-quality problems and what can be done to improve quality than is commonly suggested on the lecture circuit or in the literature. The tendency is for speakers and writers to focus on top managers (who have the clout to lead cultural shifts) and first-line employees (who directly perform services for customers). But, as we have shown, middle managers are in the center of everything and can either put fuel or sand in the gas tank. This is why one of the most critical internal services top management performs in the organization is promoting the right people into middle management, to be in charge of other people.

First-Line Service Providers

When service providers do not provide the quality of service that management asks them to provide—Gap 3 in the service-quality model —it is because they are unwilling and/or unable to do so. Like management personnel, all first-line service providers fit somewhere in the willingness/ability to serve matrix. Unlike management personnel, however, these employees do not by and large perform an internal leadership service; instead, they are the receivers of this service, for better or for worse.

To fully understand how the willingness factor operates in service performances, one needs to recall from chapter 6 the concept of discretionary effort—the difference between the maximum amount of energy and care an individual can bring to his or her work, and the minimum amount required to avoid penalty or termination.[5] Most service jobs are high in discretionary effort content, meaning that it is up to the individual employee whether to give a 100 percent service effort or to give something substantially less.

What happens often in service organizations is that poor teamwork, role conflict, and other organizational failings discussed in chapter 6 diminish discretionary effort. It is not that American service providers are slovenly or lazy. We have found absolutely no evidence in our research of a poor work ethic in America. Rather, what happens is that new, high-energy service employees do not receive the organizational support and inspiration they need to sustain them through the inevitable travail of service work. And without the support of good leaders, good teammates, clear direction, consistent signals, and most everything else we've discussed in this book, many of these service providers lose energy and effectiveness over time even as they increase in competence. They lose the will to serve.

In organizations that benefit from strong service leadership, the difference in discretionary effort between new and experienced employees is likely to be minimal. In organizations that are poorly led, the difference is likely to be striking. Exhibit 8–2 illustrates these patterns.

Constructs discussed in chapter 6 can also have an adverse effect on employees' ability to perform the service. We have found evidence in our research of companies "force-fitting" people into jobs for which they were ill-suited because the firms were unwilling to pay more to attract qualified candidates, because many openings existed and this ruled out other considerations in filling them, or because a good understanding of the required skill set did not exist which meant that almost anyone was

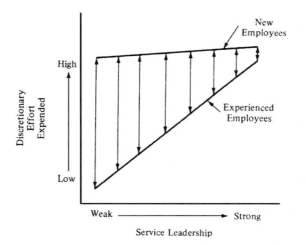

Exhibit 8–2 Difference in Discretionary Effort Expended by New and Experienced Employees

qualified. Hiring the wrong people for service jobs manifests itself in poor employee-job fit.

Moreover, service providers may not be able to properly serve their customers simply because they lack full control over the service's delivery, depending instead on other organizational units to come through for them and their customers. Perceived control is a key construct in closing Gap 3, as we have discussed.

First-line service providers—telephone installers, television repair technicians, beauticians, truck drivers, medical laboratory analysts, loan processors, accounting personnel, tax preparers, dental hygienists, secretaries, and many, many others—are often considered the root cause of America's service malaise. We disagree.

Yes, many service workers are unwilling and/or unable to meet the service expectations of their customers. But this need not be the case. If people in service roles lack the direction or the training or the support tools or the control over the service to be successful, whose fault is it? If they are hired into service roles for which they lack the basic intelligence, whose fault is it? If they are given no sense of how their role fits into the overall scheme of things, of what their customers expect, or why their work is important, whose fault is it?

The success or failure of first-line service providers is influenced greatly by the quality of service leadership they receive. When managers lead, service excellence is within reach. When managers do not, excellent service is a pipe dream. This is why we make such a fuss about leadership in this book. And this is why in the next section we focus on what management needs to do.

GUIDELINES FOR GETTING STARTED

Changing the mind-sets, habits, skills, and knowledge of human beings—which is what most organizations must do to materially improve service—is no small challenge. It involves undoing what exists—clearing out impediments to change—not only creating what does not exist. No magic formulas, simple solutions, or quick-fixes exist to get started and make headway. Overnight service-quality miracles are more a figment of lecture-circuit rhetoric than organizational reality. The truth is that it usually takes longer to materially improve service than the sponsors of this change anticipate, and then it takes longer still for the customers to notice. Quality service is a "fix" but it is almost always a "slow fix."

So in this part of the chapter we lay no claims to breakthrough thinking that will quickly raise an organization's SERVQUAL scores. Instead, we discuss some practical necessities for giving an organization a decent chance to move forward on quality. What follows are guidelines to build a *foundation for change*.

GET READY TO WORK HARD

Redirecting an organization's paths of habit and convenience is very hard work. If senior managers are to assume the mantle of service leadership, they best be prepared to work at it. Senior managers cannot delegate responsibility for service-quality improvement; they themselves must lead the charge or nothing will happen.

As Corning CEO Houghton puts it: "You almost have to have a messianic view of this. You must be willing to travel, to go and see people and talk. You can't communicate or show your commitment on a videotape or in written form all the time. You have got to believe."[6]

Consider the case of a CEO with whom we work. He runs an automobile services company, the biggest in its field, and the largest subsidiary of its parent firm. The CEO has been on the job about a year and is anxious to improve service quality to better differentiate his firm from competitors, and to command premium prices in an increasingly cutthroat pricing environment. He thinks improved service is absolutely essential and yet he faces a very complex service process (with many functions touching the service before it gets to the customer), employee morale problems traceable in part to a poorly handled reduction in force several years prior, and tremendous needs for upgraded technology. All the while, he confronts hungry, price-cutting competitors on the one hand, and a corporate parent with high profit expectations on the other hand.

Our CEO friend is very determined on the service-quality issue, having moved aggressively to open lines of communication with employees, commission research, and fund a series of specific quality-improvement projects. Progress is slow and the pressures just outlined are ever present. Does our CEO friend have a hard road to travel? You bet he does! And this is why the willingness-to-lead factor discussed earlier is so critical. Without this CEO's personal resolve, the entire service-improvement effort in his company would have crashed by now.

One of the leading academics in the service-quality field, Professor Ben Schneider of the University of Maryland, makes the hard work point well:

Service is not as mushy and touchy-feely as it has been made out to be; the delivery of consistently excellent service . . . requires the kind of hard work any business requires—hard work in mapping out responsibilities, hard work in mapping out people needs for training and superior leadership and management, hard work in designing the kinds of equipment and software service deliverers require, and hard work in identifying, continuously, customer requirements and wants. The biggest challenge is a change in mindset from easy countables . . . to measuring what is important.[7]

The superb service companies we have studied over the years all have two things in common: a good service idea and a willingness to work incredibly hard to make the idea work. Highly successful service companies do something that is important to customers, and they do it better than their competitors. As consultant G. Lynn Shostack likes to say, delivering truly superb service, day after day after day, is a bitch.

It is claimed that the average life span of a piece of trash on the grounds of Disney World is four seconds. We do not know if this statistic is absolutely true. So we shall be conservative and say that the figure is less than 30 seconds. The point is, what this company has done over the years in transforming customers into "guests in a fantasyland" is the result of obsessive dedication and commitment to the founder's dream. It was not magic that built the Magic Kingdom, it was the grind of hard work.

BASE DECISIONS ON DATA

We can offer no better advice on getting started in service improvement than to start with data. The potential effectiveness of a service-quality journey critically hinges on accurately answering the questions posed in the process model for quality improvement we presented in exhibit 3–7. So much depends on decision makers knowing what customers expect from the service, what customers perceive the service to be, and what is getting in the way of the organization meeting customers' expectations.

Without empirically based answers to these questions, the likelihood of wrong decisions and wasted resources is very great. Individual biases, assumptions, and games playing are likely to rule service-improvement planning in the absence of data. In matters of service quality, there is no substitute for knowing what is going on.

As suggested earlier, one of the biggest psychological hurdles for executives to clear in starting a service-improvement effort is the sheer magnitude of the challenge. So many customers to serve. So many transactions every day. So many employees to reach. So many different services to perform. So many "fail points" for each of the services. So many bad past decisions to overcome. So many contrary pressures to reconcile.

The best way to cope with the overwhelming part of getting started is to be selective in what is done rather than try to do everything all at once. And this requires information—information concerning (1) what target markets desire most from the service; (2) how well the firm serves these wants compared to competitors; and (3) the causes of service weaknesses that need to be corrected. This type of information gives executives a basis for prioritizing and sequencing service-improvement actions. And in doing so, the information contributes to executives' willingness and ability to provide service leadership.

Within the framework of service-quality research as we have discussed it in this book, there is another consideration in setting priorities for service interventions. This is the identification of what Berry, Bennett, and Brown call lighthouses for change—specific service initiatives that are most likely to have a positive, timely, and visible impact in focusing organizational attention on the potential for quality.[8] Some early successes in the service-improvement process, when the credibility of the effort is most at risk, can pay rich dividends in getting the attention of reluctant senior and middle managers. In general, funding decisions should favor the projects and people most likely to succeed—which requires sensitive antennae that come from information gathering.

Here are four guidelines to keep in mind in implementing a data-before-decision approach to improving service quality:

1. *Use a portfolio of research methods.* Every service research methodology has weaknesses and limitations; it is wise to use multiple methods to transcend the weaknesses of any one approach and to provide richer, more comprehensive insight. We recommend using both qualitative research (e.g., customer focus groups and managers regularly phoning customers for feedback) and more quantitative methods (e.g., expectation/perception research, "mystery" shopping of service providers, and surveying customers soon after they have received service).

2. *Do ongoing research.* Data start to get old as soon as they are collected. Any study of service gives a "snapshot" for a particular time period. It is only when these snapshots are taken regularly, when they can be lined up side-by-side, that they tell a story of patterns and trends. SERVQUAL and the other research approaches discussed in this book should be administered on a regular basis so that data patterns can be evaluated and emerging concerns spotted quickly. The right way to start a service-improvement initiative is to install an ongoing service research process, not just do a single study.

3. *Do employee research.* Often overlooked in service research is the importance of employee research. This is a serious oversight as employee research is just as critical as customer research because employees are customers, too. Who other than employees can assess the quality of internal services? Moreover, no one has a better vantage point for identifying obstacles to service than the very employees performing the service on a daily basis.

In our own research with employees, we have used with great success two key questions as part of a broader group of questions:

- What is the biggest problem you face day in and day out trying to deliver a high quality of service to your customers?
- If you were president of this company for one day, and could make only one decision to improve quality of service, what decision would you make?

We can suggest no questions that are more important to ask employees when starting a service-improvement effort than these two. These questions cut through the surface issues, exposing some of the most serious service impediments in the organization.

4. *Share research with employees.* Service research is not only valuable in guiding managerial decision making, it is also valuable in guiding first-line employee decision making. Our data show that managers had a better grasp of customers' service expectations and priorities than did first-line customer-contact employees. We do not know for sure why we found this, but one plausible explanation is that the companies we studied do considerable service-quality research which is shared with managers but not first-line employees. Because service employees are more likely to meet customers' service expectations if they first understand these expectations, we urge that service research be shared with employees. This could entail using videotaped customer focus-group sessions in employee training, issuing to employees periodic research summaries written in lay language, and even involving employees in data collection—for example, interviewing customers on the telephone.

We advise treating first-line service providers as though they were management when it comes to sharing service-quality research. It is better to be generous with information than stingy. Otherwise, employees may not know what they are supposed to do, or why they need to do it.

ORGANIZE FOR CHANGE

A readiness to work hard at quality improvement and data to guide the work are two critical pieces of the getting started puzzle. A structure that can harness energy and facilitate change is a critical third piece. Knowing what to do and being ready to do it are insufficient in and of themselves; organizing systems for replacing inertia with action must also be created. If well conceived, these organizing systems enhance both the willingness and the ability of managerial and first-line service employees to improve service.

Successful efforts in organizing for service improvement at companies such as American Express, Metropolitan Life, and National Westminster Bank USA, suggest the following principles:

1. Create service improvement roles. Casual, "let's-get-together-when-we-can-talk-about-service-quality" initiatives fail. Most people in organizations are already busy and preoccupied with their main responsibilities. And if this wasn't true a few years ago, it is true now given the belt-tightening, layoffs, and restructurings that many U.S. companies underwent in the late 1980's.

For service improvement to have a chance, it has to become part of people's main responsibilities and this means creating formal and informal organizational roles for people to perform. Formal roles might include membership in one type or another service-improvement group. A good example of formalizing service-improvement roles comes from Metropolitan Life's quality improvement process. In this process, Met Life's management asked each organizational unit to identify the principal services it delivered and the customers for these services. Once a unit's major services were identified, a quality-improvement team was established for each service with the mandate of assessing and improving it. Each team was headed by a member of middle management and made up of representatives from every organizational unit involved in creating the final service. Ultimately all the people in the company were formally involved in a quality-improvement team.[9]

Informal roles could involve being a service defender or service champion. *Service defenders*, typically respected senior line executives, protect the culture-change process from the naysayers, resistors, and budget cutters; the defenders give credibility, substance, and clout to the service-improvement effort. They make it clear that excellent service is "the way it's going to be." *Service champions* are those who actually plan, steer, coordinate, and nurse the change process; they are the heads of service-improvement units (from task forces or committees to actual departments) who provide the inspiration, energy, and cohesion required to transform talk into action. The service defender and service champion roles are both essential prerequisities to substantive cultural change. Sometimes the defender and champion roles are performed by the same person; more often, they are performed by different people.[10]

2. *Create an integrative mechanism.* One constant in virtually all successful service-improvement case studies we have examined is a high-level, interdepartmental steering group to energize, manage, and coordinate the service-improvement effort. Comprised mostly of line executives who retain their respective positions in the organization, these groups provide an ongoing mechanism for generating, evaluating, and recommending service-improvement ideas organizationwide, and for bringing cohesion to the service-improvement process. The interdepartmental makeup of these groups provides the opportunity for systemic solutions to service problems; their high-level members provide collective power to get things done (for example, getting proposals funded); their continuing presence provides an organizational rudder around which additional service-improvement entities can emerge.

It is crucial to drive service-improvement efforts from the line, not just the staff, for reasons of organizational credibility, clout, and ownership. Although a staff service-quality department may work in tandem with a service-quality steering group in implementing research, training, communications, and other initiatives, the staff function cannot replace the steering group. After all, if the staff "owns" the service-improvement process, why should line executives (or anyone else) be interested?

3. *Develop a statement of direction.* One of the principal functions of the service-quality steering group is to develop a strategic sense of what needs to be done in the company to improve service. This involves a realistic assessment of the present and a definition of what is needed in the future.

One large U.S. bank with which we are familiar has committed this appraisal to one sheet of paper, an adaptation of which is shown in exhibit 8–3. This document is helpful in capturing the direction the bank needs to take, and offering criteria by which service-improvement proposals can be evaluated.

To get started in service improvement, we recommend preparing a succinct, written statement of direction that can be a continuing guidepost for the service-related decisions that follow. The document need not be in the form or cover the particular categories of the exhibit. However, the document should be strategic rather than tactical, long term in focus rather than short term, and grounded in empirical assessment rather than based on a few people's assumptions or opinions. A good starting point for drafting a statement of direction is a research-based assessment of the various service-quality gaps present in the organization and the key causes underlying these gaps.

Exhibit 8–3 Sample Service-Quality Statement of Direction

Strategy	Achieve competitive advantage through superior customer service.	
	Now	**Needed**
Structure	Hierarchical/bureaucratic	Flat/decentralized
	Independent	Collaborative
	Market oriented	Market oriented
Style	Competition	Teamwork and
	Upward delegation	collaboration
	Variable, Random	Downward delegation
		Consistent, Reliable
Shared Values	One-way	Two-way
	communication	communication
	Confusion re: tradeoffs	Stakeholder balance
	"Life's too short"	Superior/excellent
	Risk-aversion	service
		Innovation/creativity
Staff	Weak, unseasoned	Strong managers and
	managers	leaders
	Survivor ethic	Professional ethic
Skills	Credit evaluation	Financial markets
	Product specialist	expertise
	Financial management	Relationship managers
		Sales/marketing
		management
Systems	Profit center emphasis	Customer
	Incongruent with	information/profits
	strategy	Congruent with
	Reinforce competition	strategy
	and lack of trust	Reinforce teamwork
	Control oriented	and trust
		Support oriented

4. *Involve many and emphasize teamwork.* The right way to approach the service-improvement challenge is to get as many people involved as possible and to get them involved in *teams.* Our research clearly shows the importance of teamwork in improving service, as we pointed out in chapter 6. For one thing, involvement in a team is renewing, stimulating, invigorating. The concept of a team raises the ante for individual performance. To let down the boss is bad, but to let down the team is often

worse. The aggressive use of service-improvement teams unleashes one of the most potent of all motivators—the recognition and respect of peers when one does well, and their disdain when one does poorly.

The concept of service teams is important in another respect and this is that people in organizations depend on one another to deliver an excellent service. The service process normally involves a chain of related services and servers; service quality is rarely the sole result of isolated, individual action. Feinberg and Levenstein make the point well:

> The weak links in an organization are usually at the point where departments are supposed to meet. It's at these joints that institutional arthritis attacks. When departments are separated like national frontiers, fully equipped with barbed-wire fences, bristling watchtowers, and buried mine fields, serious losses occur.[11]

In getting started on service improvement, organizations need to emphasize the development of *vertical teams* (people performing different services that contribute to the overall service) and *project or solution teams* (people who come together to solve specific problems) in addition to *horizontal teams* (people performing the same type of services).

Building a sense of service teamwork into a culture involves many of the concepts already touched on in this book. Teams have to be able to meet and exchange information on a regular basis, they need to celebrate their victories and learn from their defeats, they need recognition and reinforcement, and they need leadership from within and from above. Teamwork is a high-octane fuel for the service-quality journey; there is no better energy source than the team.

5. *Think evolution rather than revolution.* Organizational theorist Karl Weick observes that because we tend to define social problems in such grand terms (for example, the drug problem or the national debt) we paralyze our ability to act. The problem appears to be so big that we either freeze up at the enormity of the issue or we become apathetic.[12] Weick's observation is germane in the present context. As mentioned earlier in the chapter, the complexity and enormity of the service-quality challenge often inhibits management's willingness to act.

An antidote to this problem is to take the approach of steady improvement rather than breakthrough change. Improving service becomes a more inviting challenge, a more practical endeavor when one breaks big problems into little problems and seeks continuous improvement.

Developing a service-minded culture must be an evolutionary process. Revolution breeds fear and skepticism; evolution signals determination and commitment. A steady, unwavering, systematic, multifaceted approach to service improvement in which people can get their hands around definable issues and produce results is the best way to move from paralysis to action.

For the last several years, National Westminster Bank USA has had more than 100 quality-action teams, comprised of employees at all levels of the organization, working to improve quality for specific services and functions in the company. As a result, Nat West USA has reduced missorts in the mail room, reduced the error rate on applications of all types generated from the bank's 130 plus branches, improved the timeliness of operations for such services as letters of credit, reduced ATM downtime, eliminated unnecessary paperwork, improved response time to inquiries, improved fee capture, and reduced float losses.[13] Nat West executives Howard Deutsch and Neil Metviner write:

> People are getting involved, improving their own functions, cutting out the "hassles" that get in their way and looking at bettering each aspect of their jobs. Managers are finding more time to manage, motivate and develop the talents of their staffs by reducing the time spent on rework and "fire fighting." . . . People are seeing that they can make a difference, that their suggestions can become reality and that they will be rewarded and recognized for these achievements.[14]

Leverage the Freedom Factor

One of the most potent ways to get started on the service-quality journey is to "thin the rule book." Many service organizations operate with thick policy and procedure manuals that have the effect of strangling service initiative and judgment. These thick manuals benefit neither customer nor service provider, producing a regimented service when a flexible one is needed, a by-the-book service when a by-the-customer one is required.

Too many policies and procedures take the fun out of serving. For one thing, delivering inflexible service when the situation calls for flexible service angers customers and interacting with angry customers is no fun for employees. Also problematic is the frustration many employees feel when they know certain operating procedures keep them from doing good jobs in serving their customers. Which of you reading this book would relish not being able to do what you know is right for the customer and the business because to do it might result in a reprimand, penalty, or even the loss of your job?

Many service firms are unwittingly tying their employees up in knots, saying to them with the thick rule books that they are supposed to be robot servers rather than thinking servers. And in the process, these firms are reducing employees' perceived control and sapping their willingness and ability to serve customers effectively. Why on earth would a company's management choose to operate in such a dysfunctional way? Often, it is for the worst of reasons:

- because many managers do not trust employees' judgment, they make all kinds of rules that in effect represent management's judgment; and
- because thinking employees appear to threaten management prerogatives, control, and power.

To jump-start quality improvement, managers have to give back to service providers the freedom to serve that they have unnecessarily and unproductively taken away from them. Managers have to select their people well, provide them with a strong foundational culture in which to work, offer them strategic direction, and equip them with the company-specific skills and knowledge they need to perform their roles. And then the managers need to get out of the way, so the people can get the job done. Managers cannot make the transition to leadership as long as employees are so bundled in red tape that they cannot follow the lead.

We do recognize that some rules are necessary in organizational life and that certain policies need to be consistent across organizational units. Indeed, inconsistencies across service-delivery units in the same organization can create Gap 4 problems, as noted in chapter 7. We do believe service providers need boundaries and they certainly need direction. What we are advocating to help get the service improvement process started is empowerment, a concept we discussed at length in chapter 6 as it is crucial in ongoing gap management. It is also crucial for getting started.

Empowerment simply means removing the barriers that prevent workers from exercising judgment and creativity in performing their work.[15] We agree with Robert Waterman when he writes: "When managers guide instead of control, the sky's the limit on what people can accomplish."[16]

We recommend that organizations appoint one or more task forces to systematically review existing policies and procedures for the express purpose of revising or eliminating those that unnecessarily restrict service providers' freedom of action.

We recommend also that companies tackle head-on the issue of empowerment in the education and training of senior and middle managers. Managers need to learn about the dangers of overmanagement; they need to learn to ask their subordinates for ideas, widen the solution boundaries for their people, and walk away from decisions for which they are not needed.[17] Managers need to learn the freedom lesson of A. S. Neill who advises: "Think of your role as that of a release valve, not that of a restraining force. We need more green flags and less yellow; more rivers and less dams."[18]

SYMBOLIZE SERVICE QUALITY

Still another key to getting started on the service journey is the use of symbols—sayings, objects, behaviors, stories—that convey management's commitment to quality. Although symbols alone will not change a company's culture, they can reinforce shifts in organizational structure, operating policies, and performance measurement and reward systems, collectively signaling to employees that what is occurring is real.

Indeed, much of what we have covered already in this book (from the types of on-the-job behaviors that are measured to the tone and thickness of the rule book) are themselves highly symbolic, communicating to employees what is really important in the organization. Our intent in this section is to go beyond the symbolic importance of management actions that have been taken for other reasons and to discuss the importance of symbolization for its own sake.

Symbols in organizations communicate volumes to employees, including those symbols that are unintended by management and damaging. It is better to manage symbolization than not, better to think about and plan the organization's symbolic message system than leave it to chance and hope for the best.

The symbolization of quality can come in many forms, from polishing the lobby floor in The Friendly Bank daily to picking up the trash at Disney World instantly, from putting the store manager's office near the checkout area so that managers are close to the action, as is done at Randall's Food and Drugs, to featuring the most outstanding service employees in the company's annual report, as is done at Norwest Bank.

Examples of the proactive use of symbols to reinforce service-mindedness abound. Alliance Fund Services begins staff meetings with "story telling" in which participants discuss recent examples of excellent service from their respective units. National Westminster Bank USA has created a cartoon character named DIRF (an acronym for Do It Right First) who appears on employee posters, key rings, memo pads, and a variety of other internal media. A fable titled "The Legend of DIRF" was sent to the bank staff.[19]

We have found no company, however, that has been more proactive in service symbolization than Sewell Village Cadillac, a Dallas company that consistently ranks among the top U.S. Cadillac dealerships in customer satisfaction ratings and sales volume. Sewell Village displays a "leader board" that lists the top service technicians as judged by customer feedback, posts in the lunchroom service-quality scores for each technician, and awards technicians gold medallions for display at their work stations and badges for their uniform sleeves in recognition of error-free service. The floors in the repair and maintenance areas of the facilities are spotless, as clean and polished as in a well-run bank or department store. In most automobile dealerships, the sales manager makes far more money than the service manager, but at Sewell Village the service manager earns on the same level as the sales manager. In most automobile dealerships, the employees who park and retrieve cars brought in for servicing are called "lot lizards." At Sewell Village they are called customer-service representatives.

Using symbols to foster and reinforce a service ethic can encourage strong discretionary effort by adding meaning to people's work. From bank tellers to automobile mechanics, the prospect of being defeated by the rigors and grind of the service role with an accompanying loss of discretionary effort is ever present. Effective service symbols present an honest reflection of management's service commitment, appear in multiple internal media, and are ongoing, imaginative and fun. These service symbols can help recharge employees' batteries, challenge them to greater efforts, and serve as a constant reminder of the service priority.

PROMOTE THE RIGHT PEOPLE TO MANAGEMENT POSITIONS

Getting started on the service-quality journey—and then keeping going—is, in the final analysis, a result of leadership. Leadership is the only engine that can transform organizations from service mediocrity to service excellence—a point that we have not been shy about making. It follows that one of the surest ways to nurture service improvement in an organization is to identify those individuals with the strongest service leadership potential for promotion opportunities.

Earlier in the chapter we discussed the common tendency in organizations to overlook service leadership potential when promoting people into middle-management positions. This leads to the wrong people being put in charge right in the heart of the organization.

Distinguishing leaders from managers requires conscious effort. On the surface, they may look quite alike. Here are two tests to apply in identifying leaders:

1. *The footprints-in-the-sand test.* With people, the best predictor of the future is the past. The key is to study a person's past qualitatively, not just quantitatively, and to examine methods not just outcomes. Some of the key questions to ask and answer are:

   - What are the person's greatest career accomplishments—and why?

   - When in positions of authority, what innovations or new directions did this person sponsor?

   - What is this person's philosophy of service? What evidence exists that this individual can be a service champion or service defender? What evidence exists that this person is obsessive about service?

   - Do signs exist that this person inspires others and builds followership? Do others believe in this individual? Do they believe in his or her integrity?

   - Is there evidence of informal leadership in this person's background, that is, the ability to influence a group without the benefit of an official position or title?

2. *The stand-for-something test.* True leaders are determined pursuers of their vision for the future. They are clear about the direction they wish to go and why. They do not straddle the fence, are not wishy-washy, do not play it safe. As Peter Drucker has written, the leader's first task is to be the trumpet with a clear sound.[20] Thus, a crucial leadership test is the extent to which an individual's beliefs and priorities are on the table, visible for all to see.

When individuals with service leadership values and capability advance in the organization, three good things occur. First, these people have more of a chance to help the firm improve service by virtue of their greater responsibilities. Second, they get the chance to develop their leadership capabilities further. Third, as they progress in the organization, others see for themselves that service leadership is winning behavior.

One of the most important ways that top management can exercise service leadership is to replace incomplete, incorrect, or superficial criteria with leadership-based criteria and a willingness to do some digging when promoting people into middle-management positions. Otherwise, middle managers may be the black hole we wrote about earlier, thwarting the *initiatives* of senior management and the *initiative* of first-line employees.

SUMMARY

It is far easier to talk about improving service than to actually improve it. To improve service, three levels of employees—top managers, middle managers and first-line service providers—have to be willing and able to improve the services they provide.

Many firms are struggling to get started in service improvement because they lack a foundation for service-oriented cultural change and the old culture refuses to die. To build this foundation for change, top management must provide a strong internal leadership service. If top management is willing and able to do this, then the other pieces of the getting started puzzle start to fall into place; if top management is unwilling and/or unable to lead the charge, then it is unlikely that attitudes and behavior at the middle-management and first-line levels will change materially.

Chapters 4 through 7 suggest a critical role for top management in the ongoing process of service gap management; in this chapter we make the case for top management's active involvement in getting started in service improvement. Exhibit 8–4 summarizes the key steps.

These prescriptions apply to middle managers, too, and they certainly affect first-line service providers; but, in all cases, they require the support and involvement of senior management. It is up to management to get things started.

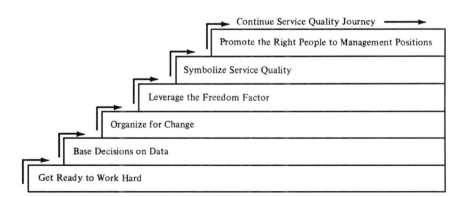

Exhibit 8–4 Steps Necessary for Getting Service-Quality Improvement off the Ground

9

◊ ◊ ◊

SERVICE-QUALITY CHALLENGES FOR THE 1990'S

WE $HAVE$ $WRITTEN$ this book to share the purposes, nature, and findings of our ongoing service-quality research sponsored by the Marketing Science Institute. In this volume we have discussed the critical importance of quality service, defined its salient dimensions, introduced the SERVQUAL methodology for measuring service quality, and used our gaps model to frame a discussion on service-quality problems and solutions. We have also presented our ideas about how firms can get started on the service-quality journey.

In this, our final chapter, we look ahead to the new decade and pose four challenges that are particularly important to closing service-quality gaps:

- designing quality into the service;
- making technology a servant;
- attacking the labor shortfall;
- raising our service aspirations.

DESIGNING QUALITY INTO THE SERVICE

One of the key service-quality challenges for the 1990's is service design. Service design is a form of architecture that involves processes rather than bricks and mortar.[1] The idea is to design high quality into the service system from the outset, to consider and respond to customers' expectations in designing each element of the service.

The quality of virtually any service depends on how well myriad elements function together in the same service process to meet customers' expectations. These elements include people who perform various services that relate to the overall service, equipment that supports these performances, and the physical environment in which the services are performed.

Design flaws in any part of a service system can and do play havoc with service quality. As college professors we can relate many stories of how elements in our educational service system have detracted from the quality of our teaching service. These include swivel classroom seats that squeak whenever students shift position (which is often) and classroom lighting systems designed to be turned totally on or off (with no dimming option for using visuals). Shostack writes:

> Every detail in the overall design is important and can affect the service encounter. I have seen corporate reputations undone by envelopes containing confidential customer data that popped open in transit due to inferior glue. I have seen computer programs changed to improve operations efficiency, with the result that statements became impossible for customers to understand.[2]

Designing quality into service requires melding the precision of the engineer, the holistic view of the architect, and the customer-mindedness of the marketer. We need to be more rigorous, more detail-oriented and more comprehensive in the design of services. Indeed, to truly design quality into a service, one needs not only to understand the customer, but one needs also to understand the service!

SERVICE BLUEPRINTING

The most promising tool for service design is "service blueprinting." Although Shostack wrote about service blueprinting as early as 1984, few organizations actually used this tool during the 1980's.[3] The real opportunity for blueprinting lies ahead.

A service blueprint is a visual definition of a service process. It displays each subprocess (or step) in the service system, linking the various steps in the sequence in which they appear. A service blueprint is essentially a detailed map or flow chart of the service process.

Two concepts used in service blueprints are especially helpful in improving quality; they are "lines of visibility" and "fail points." The line of visibility in a service blueprint separates those processes visible to the customer from those that are behind the scenes. What is important about this concept is the need to understand the interconnection between "below-the-line" and "above-the-line" service processes and to recognize that the latter processes that customers experience directly are dependent in part on the former processes that customers do not experience. Attention must be paid to designing quality into the service below the line of visibility even though customers are frequently unaware of these processes.[4] Shostack's example of a company purchasing inferior glue resulting in confidential correspondence coming open in transit illustrates the below-the-line, above-the-line connection.

Fail points are the processes in the service system where deficiencies are most likely to occur. Identifying fail points in a service blueprint focuses attention on the need for special training, additional inspection, building in corrective subprocesses, or even redesign of the original process. Reducing the vulnerability in a service system is one of the most important objectives of service design.

Hard but Worthwhile Work

Service blueprinting is slow, laborious, painstaking work. And yet the benefits are well worth the effort. The very act of creating a service blueprint provides rich insight into the service and ways to improve it. By breaking down the service process into its key elements, blueprinting also facilitates the setting of appropriate service standards for the performance of each element.

What is ideal is to blueprint new service concepts as they are being developed. The best way to design quality into a service is to do it as the service is first taking shape.

Consider, for example, the mundane subject of hotel room bathrooms. The best time to think of all the design details that make the bathroom truly workable for hotel guests is before the hotel is built. This is the optimum time to design a clothing hook for the bathroom door, a hand towel rack close to the sink, a bath towel rack close to the shower, shower curtains that are wide and long enough to keep the floor from getting soaked, and a countertop near the sink that is big enough to accommodate a toiletry kit and hair dryer. To think of these details after the hotel opens means frustrating many guests and possibly having to invest in expensive retrofits.

Although blueprinting is most ideal for designing brand new services, it is also a valuable tool for redesigning quality into existing services. As long as the service is still being offered, it is not too late to map out the service, understand it better, and correct design flaws.

Consider, for example, traditional compensation systems that pay life insurance agents generous rewards for generating new business and skimpy rewards for servicing existing business. These systems, we believe, are seriously flawed, manufacturing for life insurance agents the sales-versus-service role conflict discussed in chapter 6. The agent that conscientiously serves existing clients with information updates, annual policy review sessions, and attention to special requests (such as beneficiary changes) may not make nearly the income of agents who spend the vast majority of their time seeking new clients. Of course, in the long run service-minded agents benefit from favorable word-of-mouth advertising if—and it is a big if—they can survive during the early years.

Life insurance companies need to redesign agent performance measurement and reward systems to encourage excellent service to existing clients, a step that some companies such as Metropolitan Life and Jefferson-Pilot Life Insurance Company are already taking. Changing such a culturally entrenched system is not easy, but to not change it commits the industry to a future of client dissatisfaction, unnecessarily high rates of dropped policies, credibility/image problems, and high agent turnover rates.

One of the challenges for the 1990's, then, is to consider service quality to be a design issue. With rigorous, detailed attention to customers' expectations for each step in a service process, it is possible to design quality into the service. It is possible to eliminate or compensate for service fail points, and more intelligently link up subprocesses by combining solid understanding of customers and service in the same design exercise. The most customer-minded executives need to come off the sidelines and become directly involved in the technical design of services. And in so doing, they need to adapt some of the methods of engineers and architects. In service quality, a picture can be worth a thousand words.

MAKING TECHNOLOGY A SERVANT

Another challenge for the 1990's is to more fully realize technology's potential as a powerful service ally. It is often tempting, and sometimes chic, to view technology as a service evil. Heartless computers spew out form letters, foul up billing statements, and even answer the telephone. And the so-called personal touch seems to get lost in the shuffle.

In truth, technology, wisely conceived and used, is a liberating force that makes possible better service. The right technology used in the right way is integral to delivering the dimensions of service that customers expect: tangibles, reliability, responsiveness, assurance, and empathy. Merrill Lynch's Cash Management Account with its automated funds-shifting capability and its integrated, all-on-one-page statement—one of the most successful financial service innovations ever—is a product of technology. So are the bar-code scanners that speed up checkout lines and reduce out-of-stock conditions in retail stores, the automatic teller machines that make it easier for users to access their deposit accounts, and the computerized reservation systems that allow travel agents to make an airline reservation, reserve a specific seat, order a special meal, make hotel and car rental reservations, and print tickets and confirmations *in a matter of minutes!*

Although great strides in the use of technology have been made during the 1980's, the primary impetus for much of this change were the objectives of lowering costs and increasing productivity. Improved service was a spin-off benefit in some cases and a casualty in other cases. A key for the 1990's is to view technology as *a primary means for improving service.* The possibilities for the 1990's are considerable if service improvement can become a true driving force for technological innovation. We believe technology is one of the principal means for upgrading service in the new decade and it is in this spirit that we offer the following guidelines:

1. *Combine high tech with high touch.* For most service firms, the best opportunities for improving service come from combining technology and personal service, rather than stressing one over the other. Technology-based processes can reduce to seconds service functions that would require hours or days if performed manually. Technology can also offer greater accuracy and precision than even the most conscientious and talented of human beings.

Technology alone, however, is not nearly the service weapon of technology and personal service combined. Whereas a bank can improve service delivery with a network of well-located automatic teller machines, it could improve service even more by coupling the ATM network with personal bankers in various branch locations who serve assigned customers for their nonroutine banking needs. Thus, bank customers can use automatic or human tellers for their routine banking needs and a personal banker for their nonroutine needs, such as loans and investments. The service system offers customers both high-tech and high-touch service capabilities which customers will use depending on their overall preferences and their needs of the moment; for example, for cash or for financial advice. The synergy between technology and personal service provides a multiplicative impact.

Valley National Bank of Arizona's 1989 introduction of a 15-minute loan illustrates the power of tech and touch. Valley Bank's capability to deliver in 15 minutes a service that had required several days to deliver is made possible by what the bank calls integrated platform automation. The entire lending process is automated with personal computers in the branches communicating directly to the bank's mainframe computer. Personal bankers put required information into their personal computers and the computer system takes over, retrieving data from the customer's files, conducting a credit bureau check, approving the loan, even printing the documentation for the client to sign and the check. If additional review or approval is necessary, the system allows the personal banker to immediately transmit the information to a loan center where a loan officer makes the lending decision and transmits it back to the personal banker.[5]

Technology and personal service can be mutually supportive, interconnected keys to excellent service. If technology and personal service are in conflict, it is because management has put them in conflict. Properly blending technology and personal service requires understanding the service well enough to know which elements can be automated, and understanding the customer's service expectations well enough to know which service elements require the personal touch.[6]

2. *Use technology to support the service strategy.* Technology is a tool to improve service. Its potential for doing so relates directly to the clarity of the service strategy. When the strategy is unclear, the sense of which technology is needed to support the strategy is unclear, too.

To ask the question, "What is the best technology?" is to ask the wrong question. The proper question is: "What is our service strategy and how can we best use technology to implement this strategy?" Service strategy decisions should always precede technology decisions.

Consider the case of Florida Power & Light Company (FPL) and its quest for improved service reliability. Its strategy involves reducing the duration and frequency of service interruptions, a major cause of customers' complaints. Serving a part of the country that annually averages 80 days of thunderstorms with associated lightning causing service interruptions, company engineers teamed with suppliers to develop advanced surge protectors that protect transformers from lightning damage. The company has developed a sophisticated, computer-based lightning tracking system to anticipate where weather-related problems might occur and strategically position crews at these locations to quicken recovery response time. These and other initiatives have enabled FPL to reduce service unavailabiliity (customer minutes interrupted divided by customers served) from 70 minutes at year-end 1987 to 48.37 minutes at year-end 1988. The company's target for 1991 is 36.41 minutes.[7]

3. *Focus technology on the customer.* All technologies have a customer. The customer may be inside the organization or outside, but in either case a technology's success hinges on whether it adds value for its user. A successful technology may help service employees work smarter or faster. Or it may free them up from tedious chores, unleashing them to perform more creative and fulfilling service. Technologies that aid service employees usually aid external customers as well in ways ranging from faster service (due to improved productivity) to more reliable service (due to automating labor-intensive functions). Recall from chapter 6 that technology-job fit (employees having the appropriate technology to perform the service) is an important factor in influencing Gap 3. Of course, technology also benefits external customers directly, as the universal product code, automatic teller machine, and other examples used in this section illustrate.

Taking a customer-oriented approach to technology means identifying the customers for each technological initiative, learning their service expectations and perceptions, and eliciting their feedback to new technology concepts and prototypes. A new technology should be viewed as a new product; and like any new product, technology should be market-based.

No service company illustrates better the potential for improving service and profits through market-driven technology than McKesson Corporation, a pharmaceutical distribution company. Investing millions of dollars to develop an electronic data interchange capability to improve its service to ten thousand plus independent pharmacists, McKesson grew its business from $1 billion at the start of the 1980's to $6 billion at the end of the decade.

What McKesson did was develop information systems to help independents compete with drug chains in inventory management, pricing, credit, and other ways. With *Economost* and *Econoscan*, independent retailers could use a hand-held computer and optical character scanner for electronic order entry, inventory control, and shelf management. In addition, the retailers could use *Econocharge*, a store credit-card system; *Econoclaim*, a system for processing prescription information and insurance claims; *Econosure*, a business insurance policy; and *Pharmaserve*, an in-store computer system. Clearly, it would not be an easy task for a McKesson competitor to dislodge customers who are linked up to these data interchange systems.[8]

Materially improving service through technology requires an eclectic, open view to blending technology and people; a clear strategy; and a customer focus. It also requires a willingness to experiment, modify, learn from mistakes, and experience pain before gain. And it requires patient money. Some of the service sector's biggest technology winners for the 1990's—from American Airlines' Sabre reservation system to Citibank's state-of-the-art ATM network—involved huge, up-front investments in the 1970's and 1980's. Turning technology into a servant requires that management take the long view.

ATTACKING THE LABOR SHORTFALL

One of the most vexing problems for the service sector in the 1990's concerns labor-force shortfalls. The problem is very serious and cuts to the heart of the service-improvement challenge that many companies face. Not enough young people are available to do the nation's entry-level service work, and, of those available, many lack the basic required skills.

At the low-wage end of America's restaurant industry, 200,000 jobs were unfilled in 1989. Compounding the problem is a 250 percent employee turnover rate.[9] Some of the nation's top hotel chains have actually closed down wings of certain properties because they cannot hire enough maids to clean the rooms. New York Telephone Company had to test 60,000 applicants in 1987 to hire 3,000 deemed qualified to assume entry-level positions.[10]

What is occurring is a rapid expansion of service-sector jobs and an elevation of the basic and technical skills needed for these jobs just as changing demographics are shrinking the labor pool of young people who in many instances are not receiving the education they need to be marketable. In essence, we have labor shortages and labor mismatches rolled into one big, alarming problem.

Because people born between 1946 and 1964—the so-called baby boomers—have been having only about half as many children as their parents did, about 2 million fewer 16- to 24-year-olds will enter the labor force in 1995 compared to 1987. During this same period, the Bureau of Labor Statistics (BLS) expects the number of jobs available to grow by 10 percent, the vast majority in the service sector.[11]

A LABOR MISMATCH

Taking a longer view, the BLS estimates that private sector service jobs will expand by about 16 million jobs between 1988 and the year 2000. This growth alone almost equals the total number of people employed in the manufacturing sector in 1988. Significantly, many of the new service-sector jobs will be in high-skill areas such as engineering, medical technology, and computer programming, and medium-skill areas such as retail sales and financial services.[12]

The Labor Department has developed a methodology for measuring on a one-to-six scale the levels of reading, writing, and vocabulary skills required to perform a wide range of jobs. The Hudson Institute evaluated the new jobs the economy will create between 1985 and the year 2000 against these scales. The Hudson Institute concludes that more than three-fourths of the country's new workers will be at levels 1 and 2 (limited verbal and writing skills) while more than 50 percent of the new jobs available will be at levels 3 and above. For example, retail sales employees will have to function at level 3, writing up orders and reading merchandise information. The Hudson Institute estimates that only 22 percent of the new employees will be able to operate at level 3 or better.[13]

One million American youth drop out of school each year; for many urban high schools, dropout rates exceed 50 percent. One of every eight 17-year-olds is functionally illiterate.[14] Writes Pat Choate in *The High-Flex Society:* "The top third of America's young people is the best educated in the world, but the middle third is slipping into mediocrity, and the bottom third is at Third World standards."[15]

The implications of quantity and quality labor shortfalls for the service sector are sobering. For one thing, there will be great pressure on service organizations to lower their service-quality standards—which is the exact opposite of what needs to be done as we discuss in the next section. Thus, we may see Gap 2 in the service-quality model affected adversely.

We may also see growing Gap 3 problems in many companies as critical service positions either remain unfilled or are filled by people ill-equipped to perform in them. As we write this book, our impression is that the staffs of major hotels in Stockholm, Sweden, speak better English than the staffs of major hotels in New York City. In fact, this may not be quite true but it is close enough to the truth to signal the depth of the labor-pool challenge facing service firms.

THE NEED FOR INNOVATIVE APPROACHES

America's best-managed service companies are starting to deal with the labor-pool problem in innovative ways. In so doing, they are setting examples for others to follow. McDonald's established its McMasters training program in 1986 to attract more older workers into employment. McDonald's and other fast-food chains are installing self-service drink-dispensing equipment. Customers get free refills but it alleviates the need for extra employees to pour drinks.

Walt Disney World trains existing employees to recruit new employees. Each division is responsible for its own recruiting on the basis that people actually performing a job know it better than anyone else and are more likely to hire good people.[16] Wal-Mart provides scholarship assistance to employees so that they can attend colleges or universities while continuing to work part time. Successful graduates are then promoted into management. Approximately 40 percent of Wal-Mart's managers started as hourly trainees.[17]

A growing number of service companies are tackling worker skill deficiencies head-on—teaching employees to read and write. By the late 1980's, American firms were investing $300 million a year to teach employees basic skills.[18] And more corporate executives are investing their personal time and their firms' resources to assist local schools in curriculum development, teaching, equipment acquisition, and funding.

The key to this complex labor-pool puzzle is new mind-sets at the highest corporate levels. Service companies need to compete as hard for talent as they compete for market share. They need to assume direct responsibility for developing talent, for not only recruiting the best available people but also encouraging and helping them to get better once they are employed. They need to work every angle to cope with the problem, from substituting new service designs and technology for people to taking a marketing approach to recruiting through aggressive advertising, career fairs, employee-get-an-employee campaigns and more. There is no law after all that forces service companies to restrict employee recruiting to small-type ads buried in the classified sections of newspapers!

Most of all, service companies have to work harder at improving the jobs they wish to fill. It is important to think of jobs as products that employees buy and to tailor these job-products to fulfill employees' wants and needs. This is what service companies must do most of all to attract and retain employees who are able and willing to provide excellent service. Companies must seek to attract and retain a larger market share of the most qualified employment candidates through superior job-products.

No company in America better illustrates the internal marketing approach we are proposing than Walt Disney World. Disney World is at the same time a no-nonsense employer with rigorous training regimens and strict personal grooming standards for all "cast members" and a generous employer that invests heavily to create good jobs. For example, Disney World operates a 75-acre recreation complex including a lake for the exclusive use of employees and their families. The company posts available positions every week through its "Casting Call," choosing to promote from within. It publishes a weekly employee newspaper, *Eyes and Ears;* sells Disney merchandise to employees at substantial discounts; and provides continuing education classes, stock purchase plans, a housing referral service, and many other services to employees.

Everyone employed by Disney World is on a first-name basis. If Walt Disney were alive today, all employees would refer to him as "Walt."

Disney World is indeed a special place to work: a culture that attracts good people and spurs their achievement, satisfaction, and enjoyment on the job. As Walt Disney once said himself, "You can dream, create, design and build the most wonderful place in the world . . . but it takes people to make the dream a reality."[19]

RAISING OUR SERVICE ASPIRATIONS

The most significant service challenge of them all for the 1990's is to raise our service aspirations. It is time for American executives to declare war on service mediocrity, to become indignant in the face of shoddy service, intolerant in the face of so-so service.

If the 1980's were a decade of growing service consciousness in America, the 1990's must be the decade in which we decide collectively, as executives and as consumers, to seek superior service, to settle for nothing less, to be more determined, more obsessive, more committed than ever before.

The stakes are very high. It is more than a matter of economics although the issue of economic superiority within industries and among countries is at stake. It is also a matter of national pride. The rising clamor for better service in America is reflected in developments ranging from cover stories in national magazines to legislation requiring airlines to publish their on-time performance records. This is really a clamor to return to the country's roots of craftsmanship, integrity, generosity, and civility. The service issue, so visible and so much a part of everyone's everyday, seems to have become a barometer of a declining culture.

Roger Hale, the chairman of Tennant Company, a manufacturer of industrial floor cleaning equipment, was recently named Minnesota's Executive of the Year in recognition of his company's commitment to quality. In explaining his obsession for quality, Hale exposes the cultural challenge we face as a country.

> Tennant Company was known for producing top-quality floor maintenance equipment. But during my visits with our Japanese joint-

venture partner in the late 1970's, I had been hearing complaints—sometimes bitter—about hydraulic leaks in our most successful machines. Back home, I began asking questions: Why were the hydraulic leaks happening only in the machines we sent to Japan? . . . As it turned out, the leaks weren't just happening in Japan. The difference was that U.S. customers accepted the leaks. If a drop of oil appeared on a freshly polished floor, they simply wiped it up.[20]

ROLE MODELS EXIST

We do have examples of American companies unwilling to play second fiddle on service quality to the Japanese or any other country. What we need now is for many executives to become zealous about service, to become as competitive concerning their quality standards as they are on other matters, such as market share and stock price. Indeed, if they become this committed to quality, market share and stock price will be favorably affected, as we discussed at the beginning of the book.

We need more companies such as Smith & Hawken, Deluxe Corporation, and Dunkin' Donuts Incorporated. Gap 2 is not a problem in these companies; if anything, the companies' service standards are higher than the customers' expectations!

Smith & Hawken is a California-based firm that sells garden products via catalog. Early on its management saw the need to overcompensate through exemplary service for the customer's perceived loss of control in purchasing by catalog. In the mid-1980's, the company codified its principles of service. The following partial list has brief explanatory notes in parentheses:

- *Our goal as a company is to have customer service that is not just the best, but legendary.* (Legendary may seem grandiose but you need a goal that is ever expanding rather than merely attainable.)
- *You are the customer.* (When a customer is upset, service personnel need to be the customer and feel the customer's unhappiness. Service personnel have permission to do whatever it will take to make the customer feel good again about the company.)
- *You are the company.* (Each employee must carry the authority, dignity, and bearing of ownership.)
- *There is no such thing as taking too much time with a customer.* (Our business lives, breathes, and dies according to one simple activity: repeat business.)

- *The phone is mightier than the pen.* (When customers have questions or concerns, we call. Calling collapses the time between problem and solution, as well as eliminates paperwork.)
- *A job isn't done until it is checked.* (If we don't build in redundancies, the customers will do our error checking for us and they may not be forgiving.)
- *Do it once and do it yourself.* (Whenever possible, one employee should follow through on the entire customer service episode.)[21]

Deluxe Corporation (formerly Deluxe Check Printers) of St. Paul, Minnesota, is one of America's most profitable companies, a success that traces back to August 18, 1936, when company founder, W. R. Hotchkiss decreed, "Starting immediately, regardless of expense, energy and effort involved, every order will be shipped by the end of the day after it arrives." Deluxe still adheres to this standard of service today, reporting its service-quality statistics in the shareholders letter appearing in its annual report. In 1988 Deluxe shipped 94.4 percent of its orders by the day-after deadline and printed 98.7 percent of them without error. So obsessed is Deluxe with service quality that it pushed legislation through Congress to allow it to put U.S. Postal Service stations inside its plants to improve average delivery time.[22]

Deluxe Corporation's obsession with being the best in its field is matched by Dunkin' Donuts' obsession with serving the best coffee to be found anywhere. The company seems to be succeeding, selling 405 million cups of coffee in the United States in 1988.[23] Here is how Clifford and Cavanaugh describe Dunkin' Donuts' obsession with making excellent coffee in the book *The Winning Performance:*

> Dunkin' Donuts really cares about the quality of its coffee. Its goal is to serve the "best cup of coffee in the world." Dunkin' Donuts has a 23-page specification of what it requires in a coffee bean. But buying high-quality, specially blended coffee beans is just the beginning. Dunkin' Donuts franchisees have to make sure their coffee is fresh. Beans are to be used within ten days of their delivery; if they are not, they are returned on the next Dunkin' Donuts supply truck. Once the coffee is brewed, it can be served for only 18 minutes; after that it must be thrown out. And the coffee must be brewed between 196 and 198 degrees Fahrenheit exactly. Dunkin' is one of the few chains that still use real cream—*not* half and half, *not* milk, *not* the sugar-based powder.[24]

From retailing garden tools to delivering checks to making coffee, superior service is within reach if we are willing to reach for it. Here are four tenets to follow in reaching for superior service:

1. *Seek constant improvement.* Service excellence is an attitude, a mind-set; it is also competence and design. The only option is to continually strive for a stronger service attitude, more competence and better design every day of every week of every month of every year.

Service quality is *not* a program; it does not have an end point. One commonality in the best-serving companies in America is a burning desire to improve, to be better next week and next year than this week and this year.

Senior managers cannot build a service-minded culture within their companies by investing in service when earnings are good and putting service issues on the back burner when earnings are poor. Executives cannot build a service-minded culture by turning the service issue on and off like a water faucet. Service excellence requires a full-court press—all of the time.[25]

2. *Forget about being a commodity business.* There is no such thing as a commodity business; rather, there are only businesses that we think of in this way. Commodity is a mind-set. Whereas some observers might consider bank checks or coffee to be commodities, executives at Deluxe Corporation and Dunkin' Donuts clearly do not and this is their competitive advantage. Executives in these companies see service excellence as the primary opportunity to differentiate their offering from competitors, as the primary means for competing on value rather than price. These executives view service quality as the one dimension of business performance that their competitors may be unable to match. They view service excellence as the opportunity to be a company in a commodity industry that does not offer a commodity.

3. *Do the service right the first time.* Our research has shown consistently that consumers consider reliability to be the single most important dimension in judging service. Consumers want service providers to look good, be responsive, be knowledgeable and nice, and be empathetic. But most of all, consumers expect service providers to perform the service they promised to perform accurately and dependably.

For most consumers, reliability is the core service. Service providers' apologies start to wear thin when a company is unreliable. When a company is careless in performing the service, when it makes frequent mistakes, when it is casual about keeping its service promises, customers lose confidence in the firm's reliability and little can be done to regain it.

Our data show our sample companies to be more deficient on the reliability dimension than on any other. These firms have the most negative SERVQUAL scores on the dimension of service quality that is most important to consumers.

American executives need to set their sights higher for service reliability. They need to place a higher premium on error-free service; they need to value zero defects and back up their conviction with resources. In service design; in the application of technology; in the goal-setting process; in the hiring, training, measuring, and rewarding of staff, executives need to keep pursuing better and better reliability. Reliability is the heart of excellent service.

4. *Do the service very right the second time.* It is sometimes suggested on the lecture circuit that it is okay for companies to be careless in the primary service as long as they are effective in solving the problems that carelessness creates. However, as our data from chapter 2 show, this notion is false. It is far better to be excellent in reliability and recovery than to be fair in reliability and excellent in recovery.

Excellent reliability and recovery represent a powerful one-two punch in service quality. Companies need to aspire to doing the service right the first time and, on those occasions when this does not occur, doing the service very right the second time.

How a company handles service problems tells consumers a great deal about the firm's service values and priorities. Customers are used to experiencing additional hassles and disappointments when attempting to resolve problems with service organizations. Thus, quick, competent, courteous problem resolution gives organizations an excellent opportunity to impress customers and recover much of—but probably not all of—the confidence lost via the original service encounter.

Being excellent in problem resolution service involves encouraging customers to communicate their problems to the company so the company has the chance to recover. It involves having enough staff, and the right kind of staff: personable, resilient, well-trained. It involves systems, structure, and authority that allow the staff to solve the problem on the first contact with the customer. It involves taking the long view toward creating true customers, rather than the short view of maximizing near-term profits.[26] Most of all, being excellent in problem resolution requires wanting to be excellent in problem resolution, viewing this as a genuine opportunity to build and improve the business rather than as a peripheral activity or necessary evil.

Seeking continuous improvement, seeking differentiation from competitors no matter which type of product is involved, combining ultrareliable service with excellent recovery—these four tenets convey collectively that even good service isn't good enough for the 1990's. It is time to raise our service standards in America and aspire to be the best servers in the world. This is the signal challenge for the new decade; the potential payoff—for companies and country—is rich indeed.

FINAL WORDS

In this chapter we have discussed four challenges for the 1990's that are especially important in closing the service-quality gaps in our model. Designing quality into the service, using technology to enhance service, attacking labor-pool shortfalls, and raising our service aspirations are all critical for the new decade.

We believe excellent service is a genuine key to a better future—for those who give service as well as for those who receive it, for companies that make things as well as for companies traditionally labeled service businesses, for our country's national pride, as well as its economic competitiveness.

This is the new age of the service economy in America and elsewhere. What kind of future is in store for our citizens, our communities, our industries, our economy, and our national self-respect if our service is slovenly, uncaring, incompetent?

The spirit of this book is that service quality need not be an amorphous or mystical idea. Through the framework of our research-based gaps model and our methodology anchored in SERVQUAL we have attempted in this volume to convey that service *is* definable, *is* measurable, *is* improvable. What is needed now in organizations is the internal service of service leadership.

Executives must assume the mantle of service leadership to inspire people to be the best they can be; give them the systems, tools, and technologies to facilitate their work; remove unnecessary obstacles and discouragements from their paths; allow them the freedom to truly serve their customers; and build internal cultures of teamwork, congruence, and achievement. Companies ranging from American Express to Federal Express, Deluxe Corporation to L. L. Bean, McKesson to Disney, are winning big with excellent service. And so can many more of our companies.

Our book's publication coincides with the onset of a brand new decade. This is perfect. The 1980's were the service-quality awareness decade in the United States. Let's make the 1990's the service-quality action decade.

APPENDIXES

I N THE FOLLOWING APPENDIXES, we discuss the approaches we have developed to quantify and analyze the five gaps in our conceptual model of service quality. Appendix A presents SERVQUAL, the instrument for measuring customer's perceptions of service quality (Gap 5), and discusses its applications. Appendix B presents approaches for quantifying Gaps 1 through 4 and the factors associated with them (i.e., their potential causes).

SERVQUAL AND ITS APPLICATIONS

S ERVQUAL is a concise multiple-item scale with good reliability and validity that companies can use to better understand the service expectations and perceptions of their customers.[1] We have designed the instrument to be applicable across a broad spectrum of services. As such, it provides a basic skeleton through its expectations/perceptions format encompassing statements for each of the five service-quality dimensions (tangibles, reliability, responsiveness, assurance, and empathy). The skeleton, when necessary, can be adapted or supplemented to fit the characteristics or specific research needs of a company.

We should also mention that we have refined the original SERVQUAL instrument based on our experience in using it in a number of studies. The instrument we present in this appendix is the latest version that has benefited from several refinements and improvements.

THE SERVQUAL INSTRUMENT

Exhibit A–1 on page 180 contains the SERVQUAL instrument. The questionnaire in exhibit A–1, in addition to containing an expectations section consisting of 22 statements and a perceptions section consisting of a matching set of company-specific statements, also contains a section to ascertain customers' assessment of the relative importance of the five dimensions. This section is placed between the expectations and perceptions sections.

In addition to including the sections in exhibit A–1, our customer questionnaire contained a section on customers' experience with, and

overall impressions about, the service (e.g., had they encountered a problem with the service, would they recommend the service to a friend) and
a section on demographics (e.g., age, sex, income, education). Depending
on the specific information needs of a company, appropriate sections like
these can be added to the basic instrument shown in exhibit A–1.

COMPUTING THE SERVQUAL GAP SCORES

The SERVQUAL statements (in both the expectations and perceptions sections) are grouped into the five dimensions as follows:

Dimension	Statements Pertaining to the Dimension
Tangibles	Statements 1–4
Reliability	Statements 5–9
Responsiveness	Statements 10–13
Assurance	Statements 14–17
Empathy	Statements 18–22

Assessing the quality of service using SERVQUAL involves computing the difference between the ratings customers assign to the paired
expectation/perception statements. Specifically, a Gap 5 or SERVQUAL
score for each statement pair, for each customer, is computed as follows:

SERVQUAL Score = Perception Score − Expectation Score

A company's quality of service along each of the five dimensions can
then be assessed across all customers by averaging their SERVQUAL
scores on statements making up the dimension. For instance, if N customers responded to a SERVQUAL survey, the average SERVQUAL
score along each dimension is obtained through the following two steps:

1. For each customer, add the SERVQUAL scores on the statements
   pertaining to the dimension and divide the sum by the number of
   statements making up the dimension.
2. Add the quantity obtained in step 1 across all N customers and
   divide the total by N.

The SERVQUAL scores for the five dimensions obtained in the preceding fashion can themselves be averaged (i.e., summed and divided by
five) to obtain an overall measure of service quality. This overall measure
is an *unweighted* SERVQUAL score because it does not take into account
the relative importance that customers attach to the various dimensions.

An overall *weighted* SERVQUAL score that takes into account the relative importance of the dimensions is obtained through the following four steps:

1. For each customer, compute the average SERVQUAL score for each of the five dimensions (this step is the same as the first step in the two-step procedure outlined earlier).
2. For each customer, multiply the SERVQUAL score for each dimension (obtained in step 1) by the importance weight assigned by the customer to that dimension (the importance weight is simply the points the customer allocated to the dimension divided by 100).
3. For each customer, add the weighted SERVQUAL scores (obtained in step 2) across all five dimensions to obtain a combined weighted SERVQUAL score.
4. Add the scores obtained in step 3 across all N customers and divide the total by N.

APPLICATIONS OF SERVQUAL

As described in the preceding section, data obtained through the SERVQUAL instrument can be used to compute service-quality gap scores at different levels of detail: for each statement pair, for each dimension, or combined across all dimensions. By examining these various gap scores a company can not only assess its overall quality of service as perceived by customers but also identify the key dimensions, and facets within those dimensions, on which it should focus its quality-improvement efforts. The SERVQUAL instrument and the data generated by it can also be used in a variety of other ways as discussed next.

COMPARING CUSTOMERS' EXPECTATIONS AND PERCEPTIONS OVER TIME

While examining SERVQUAL scores (which represent the gap between customers' expectations and perceptions) can be insightful, additional insight can be gained by tracking the levels of expectations and perceptions through repeated administration of SERVQUAL (e.g., once every six months or once a year). Such a comparison of expectations and perceptions over time reveals not only how the gap between the two is changing but also whether the changes are stemming from changing expectations, changing perceptions, or both. The illustrative chart in exhibit A–2 tracks customers' expectations and perceptions along the

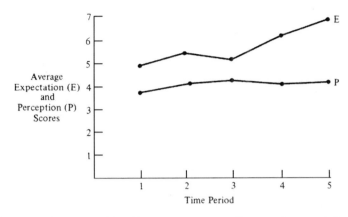

Exhibit A-2 Illustrative Tracking of Customers' Expectations and Perceptions along the Reliability Dimension

reliability dimension (similar charts can be constructed for the other dimensions). The chart shows that quality along the reliability dimension has deteriorated sharply in periods 4 and 5, apparently due to a significant increase in expectations without a corresponding improvement in perceptions.

Comparing Your Own SERVQUAL Scores Against Competitors' Scores

The two-section format of SERVQUAL, with separate expectation and perception sections, makes it convenient to measure the service quality of several competing companies simply by including a set of perception statements for each company. The expectations section need not be repeated for each company. A company can, therefore, easily adapt SERVQUAL and use it to track its quality of service against that of its leading competitors. Exhibit A-3 illustrates such competitive tracking along the reliability dimension. Similar charts constructed for the other dimensions, as well as for overall service quality, would provide valuable insights about the company's relative strengths and weaknesses and how they are changing over time.

Examining Customer Segments with Differing Quality Perceptions

One potential application of SERVQUAL is its use in categorizing a company's customers into several perceived-quality segments (e.g., high,

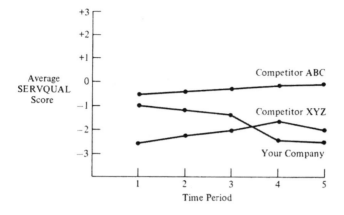

Exhibit A–3 Illustrative Tracking of SERVQUAL Scores along the Reliability Dimension

medium, and low) on the basis of their individual SERVQUAL scores. These segments then can be analyzed on the basis of (1) demographic, psychographic, and/or other profiles; (2) the relative importance of the five dimensions in influencing service-quality perceptions; and (3) the reasons behind the perceptions reported. For example, suppose a company found that a large number of SERVQUAL respondents falling in the medium perceived-quality group fit its prime target market based on demographic and psychographic criteria. Suppose further that reliability and assurance were found to be the most important quality dimensions and, based on perception-expectation gap scores for items concerning these dimensions, the items relating to record-keeping accuracy and behavior of contact personnel revealed the biggest gaps. With these data, the company's management would understand better what needs to be done to improve its image in the eyes of a very important group— customers within the company's prime target market who give the company medium service quality scores and who are in position to either respond to improved service from the company or defect to the competition.

A company might also benefit by examining the differences, if any, in the service-quality perceptions of customers segmented on the basis of demographic characteristics (e.g., sex, age, income), length of association with the company, willingness to recommend the company, and so forth. Overall SERVQUAL scores, as well as scores on individual dimensions, can be computed for each segment and compared across segments. A prerequisite for this application (and the preceding one) is inclusion in the

SERVQUAL questionnaire of questions pertaining to the relevant segmentation variables.

Assessing Quality Perceptions of Internal Customers

SERVQUAL, with appropriate adaptation, can be used by departments and divisions within a company to ascertain the quality of service they provide to employees in other departments and divisions. For instance, suppose the data processing department in XYZ Company wishes to use SERVQUAL to determine how its internal customers rate its quality of service. To do so, it can modify SERVQUAL by incorporating "excellent data processing departments" as the frame of reference throughout the expectations section and replacing "XYZ Co." with "XYZ's data processing department" in the perceptions section. The modified instrument can be administered to a sample of internal customers, or to all such customers if the data processing department's internal customer base is fairly small (e.g., 200 or less).

Exhibit A-1 SERVQUAL Questionnaire

Directions: Based on your experiences as a consumer of _____ services, please think about the kind of _____ company that would deliver excellent quality of service. Think about the kind of _____ company with which you would be pleased to do business. Please show the extent to which you think such a _____ company would possess the feature described by each statement. If you feel a feature is *not at all essential* for excellent _____ companies such as the one you have in mind, circle the number 1. If you feel a feature is *absolutely essential* for excellent _____ companies, circle 7. If your feelings are less strong, circle one of the numbers in the middle. There are no right or wrong answers—all we are interested in is a number that truly reflects your feelings regarding companies that would deliver excellent quality of service.

	Strongly Disagree						Strongly Agree
1. Excellent_____ companies will have modern-looking equipment.	1	2	3	4	5	6	7
2. The physical facilities at excellent _____ companies will be visually appealing.	1	2	3	4	5	6	7
3. Employees at excellent _____ companies will be neat-appearing.	1	2	3	4	5	6	7
4. Materials associated with the service (such as pamphlets or statements) will be visually appealing in an excellent _____ company.	1	2	3	4	5	6	7
5. When excellent _____ companies promise to do something by a certain time, they will do so.	1	2	3	4	5	6	7
6. When a customer has a problem, excellent _____ companies will show a sincere interest in solving it.	1	2	3	4	5	6	7
7. Excellent _____ companies will perform the service right the first time.	1	2	3	4	5	6	7
8. Excellent _____ companies will provide their services at the time they promise to do so.	1	2	3	4	5	6	7

(continued)

	Strongly Disagree						Strongly Agree
9. Excellent _____ companies will insist on error-free records.	1	2	3	4	5	6	7
10. Employees in excellent _____ companies will tell customers exactly when services will be performed.	1	2	3	4	5	6	7
11. Employees in excellent _____ companies will give prompt service to customers.	1	2	3	4	5	6	7
12. Employees in excellent _____ companies will always be willing to help customers.	1	2	3	4	5	6	7
13. Employees in excellent _____ companies will never be too busy to respond to customers' requests.	1	2	3	4	5	6	7
14. The behavior of employees in excellent _____ companies will instill confidence in customers.	1	2	3	4	5	6	7
15. Customers of excellent _____ companies will feel safe in their transactions.	1	2	3	4	5	6	7
16. Employees in excellent _____ companies will be consistently courteous with customers.	1	2	3	4	5	6	7

	Strongly Disagree						Strongly Agree
17. Employees in excellent _____ companies will have the knowledge to answer customers' questions.	1	2	3	4	5	6	7
18. Excellent _____ companies will give customers individual attention.	1	2	3	4	5	6	7
19. Excellent _____ companies will have operating hours convenient to all their customers.	1	2	3	4	5	6	7
20. Excellent _____ companies will have employees who give customers personal attention.	1	2	3	4	5	6	7
21. Excellent _____ companies will have the customer's best interests at heart.	1	2	3	4	5	6	7
22. The employees of excellent _____ companies will understand the specific needs of their customers.	1	2	3	4	5	6	7

Directions: Listed below are five features pertaining to _____ companies and the services they offer. We would like to know how important each of these features is to *you* when you evaluate a _____ company's quality of service. Please allocate a total of 100 points among the five features *according to how important each feature is to you*—the more important a feature is to you, the more points you should allocate to it. Please ensure that the points you allocate to the five features add up to 100.

1. The appearance of the
    _____ company's physical facilities,
    equipment, personnel, and
    communication materials.   _____ points

2. The _____ company's ability to
    perform the promised service
    dependably and accurately.   _____ points

3. The _____ company's willingness to
    help customers and provide prompt
    service.   _____ points

4. The knowledge and courtesy of the
    _____ company's employees and their
    ability to convey trust and confidence.   _____ points

5. The caring, individualized attention the
    _____ company provides its
    customers.   _____ points

    TOTAL points allocated   100   **points**

    Which *one* feature among the above five
    is *most important* to you? (please enter
    the feature's number)   _____

    Which feature is *second* most important
    to you?   _____
    Which feature is *least important* to you?   _____

Directions: The following set of statements relate to your feelings about XYZ Company. For each statement, please show the extent to which you believe XYZ Company has the feature described by the statement. Once again, circling a 1 means that you strongly disagree that XYZ Company has that feature, and circling a 7 means that you strongly agree. You may circle any of the numbers in the middle that show how strong your feelings are. There are no right or wrong answers—all we are interested in is a number that best shows your perceptions about XYZ Company.

		Strongly Disagree						Strongly Agree
1.	XYZ Co. has modern-looking equipment.	1	2	3	4	5	6	7
2.	XYZ Co.'s physical facilities are visually appealing.	1	2	3	4	5	6	7
3.	XYZ Co.'s employees are neat-appearing.	1	2	3	4	5	6	7
4.	Materials associated with the service (such as pamphlets or statements) are visually appealing at XYZ Co.	1	2	3	4	5	6	7
5.	When XYZ Co. promises to do something by a certain time, it does so.	1	2	3	4	5	6	7
6.	When you have a problem, XYZ Co. shows a sincere interest in solving it.	1	2	3	4	5	6	7
7.	XYZ Co. performs the service right the first time.	1	2	3	4	5	6	7
8.	XYZ Co. provides its services at the time it promises to do so.	1	2	3	4	5	6	7
9.	XYZ Co. insists on error-free records.	1	2	3	4	5	6	7
10.	Employees in XYZ Co. tell you exactly when services will be performed.	1	2	3	4	5	6	7
11.	Employees in XYZ Co. give you prompt service.	1	2	3	4	5	6	7
12.	Employees in XYZ Co. are always willing to help you.	1	2	3	4	5	6	7

(Continued)

		Strongly Disagree						Strongly Agree
13.	Employees in XYZ Co. are never too busy to respond to your requests.	1	2	3	4	5	6	7
14.	The behavior of employees in XYZ Co. instills confidence in you.	1	2	3	4	5	6	7
15.	You feel safe in your transactions with XYZ Co.	1	2	3	4	5	6	7
16.	Employees in XYZ Co. are consistently courteous with you.	1	2	3	4	5	6	7
17.	Employees in XYZ Co. have the knowledge to answer your questions.	1	2	3	4	5	6	7
18.	XYZ Co. gives you individual attention.	1	2	3	4	5	6	7
19.	XYZ Co. has operating hours convenient to all its customers.	1	2	3	4	5	6	7
20.	XYZ Co. has employees who give you personal attention.	1	2	3	4	5	6	7
21.	XYZ Co. has your best interests at heart.	1	2	3	4	5	6	7
22.	Employees of XYZ Co. understand your specific needs.	1	2	3	4	5	6	7

APPROACHES FOR MEASURING SERVICE-PROVIDER GAPS AND THEIR CAUSES

I N THIS APPENDIX we first describe the approach and questions we have used to quantify the extent of Gaps 1 through 4. We then present the items to measure the factors or antecedents (discussed in chapters 4–7) pertaining to each of the four gaps.

MEASURING GAPS 1 THROUGH 4

GAP 1

From a measurement standpoint, Gap 1 is different from the other three service-provider gaps because it crosses the boundary between the customer and provider sides of our conceptual model (please refer to exhibit 3–6). Specifically, its measurement requires a comparison of responses pertaining to expectations from two different samples—customers and managers. Therefore, in the latest empirical phase of our research we included the expectations section of SERVQUAL (with modified directions) along with the section for measuring the relative importance of the five dimensions, in the questionnaire we used to survey managers. These are the first two sections of the instrument shown in exhibit B–1.

As the directions for the first two sections of exhibit B–1 imply, the data generated from those sections pertain to managers' perceptions of customers' expectations and the relative importance customers attach to the five quality dimensions. The extent of Gap 1 can, therefore, be measured by determining the discrepancy between the managers' ratings and the customers' ratings on the corresponding questions on the SERV-QUAL questionnaire (exhibit A–1). Specifically, a Gap 1 score along each of the five dimensions is computed as follows:

1. Determine the average expectation score along the dimension for the customer sample. (This can be done by using a procedure similar to the two-step procedure outlined in appendix A for determining the average SERVQUAL score along each dimension.)
2. Determine the average expectation score along the dimension as perceived by the manager sample, using the same procedure as under step 1 but on data from the manager sample.
3. Subtract the average score determined in step 1 from the average score determined in step 2. The resulting difference is the Gap 1 score along the dimension (the more negative the Gap 1 score, the worse the gap).

An *overall* Gap 1 score can also be computed by first averaging the scores across the five dimensions for each sample separately and then computing the difference between the two sample averages. To compute a *weighted* overall Gap 1 score, one needs to first compute a weighted expectation score for each sample separately (using a procedure similar to the four-step procedure outlined in appendix A for computing a weighted SERVQUAL score) and then compute the difference between the two weighted sample scores. The weighted overall Gap 1 score captures the discrepancies between customers and managers on both expectations along the five dimensions and the relative importance of the dimensions.

GAPS 2 THROUGH 4

We measured Gaps 2 through 4 by asking samples of employees in the companies participating in this phase of our research to directly indicate their perceptions of the extent of those gaps. Specifically, for each gap, employee respondents used a seven-point scale to indicate the extent of the gap along each of the five service quality dimensions. The last three sections of the instrument in exhibit B–1 contain, respectively, the rating scales we used to measure gaps 2, 3, and 4. On these scales, *higher* numbers imply *smaller* gaps. An *overall* measure of each gap is obtained by averaging the scores across the five rating scales pertaining to the gap.

APPROPRIATE RESPONDENTS FOR MEASURING GAPS 1 THROUGH 4

In our gap model (shown in exhibit 3–6), Gaps 1 and 2 are managerial gaps in that the key company employees to whom they pertain are *managers*—Gap 1 stems from managers' lack of understanding of customers' expectations and Gap 2 represents managers' failure to set appropriate service specifications. Gaps 3 and 4, in contrast, pertain more to *first-line service employees* because they are the ones whose service-delivery performance may fall short of service specifications (Gap 3) and/or promises made to customers through external communications (Gap 4). Therefore, on the basis of closeness to and knowledge about the various gaps, the most appropriate survey respondents are managers for measuring Gaps 1 and 2 and customer-contact personnel for measuring Gaps 3 and 4.

In addition to obtaining the most appropriate measures of the four gaps, we also wanted to ascertain the differences, if any, between managers' and contact personnel's perceptions of all four gaps. We therefore included measures of all four gaps in both the manager and contact personnel surveys. And, as described in chapters 4 through 7, our results showed that managers had a better understanding of customers' expectations than contact personnel had (i.e., managers had a smaller Gap 1 than contact personnel), but that contact personnel's perceptions of Gaps 2, 3, and 4 were generally more optimistic (i.e., implied smaller gaps).

MEASURING ANTECEDENTS OF GAPS 1 THROUGH 4

In chapters 4 through 7, we identified, defined, and discussed a number of key factors that are potential antecedents of Gaps 1 through 4. To measure the extent to which these factors were present in the companies participating in the empirical phase of our research, we developed specific statements pertaining to the factors. We developed these statements based on information obtained from our earlier qualitative research phases and on scales available in the literature to measure several of the factors (e.g., role conflict, role ambiguity). We attached seven-point scales (ranging from Strongly Disagree to Strongly Agree) to the statements to obtain the respondents' ratings.

Exhibit B–2 contains the set of statements in the questionnaire we used to survey managers. These statements pertain to potential antecedents of the two managerial gaps (i.e., Gaps 1 and 2). The specific antecedents and statements on the questionnaire pertaining to them follow:

Antecedents of Gap 1	Corresponding Statements
Marketing research orientation	Statements 1–4
Upward communication	Statements 5–8
Levels of management	Statement 9
Antecedents of Gap 2	**Corresponding Statements**
Management's commitment to service quality	Statements 10–13
Goal setting	Statements 14–15
Task standardization	Statements 16–17
Perception of feasibility	Statements 18–20

Exhibit B–3 contains the set of statements in the questionnaire that we used to survey contact personnel. These statements pertain to potential antecedents of the two gaps representing performance shortfalls on the part of contact personnel (i.e., Gaps 3 and 4). The specific antecedents and the questionnaire statements pertaining to them follow:

Antecedents of Gap 3	Corresponding Statements
Teamwork	Statements 1–5
Employee-job fit	Statements 6–7
Technology-job fit	Statement 8
Perceived control	Statements 9–12
Supervisory control systems	Statements 13–15
Role conflict	Statements 16–19
Role ambiguity	Statements 20–24
Antecedents of Gap 4	**Corresponding Statements**
Horizontal communication	Statements 25–28
Propensity to overpromise	Statements 29–30

DETERMINING SCORES FOR THE ANTECEDENTS OF GAPS 1 THROUGH 4

The average score for each antecedent (on a scale of 1 to 7 on which the higher the score the more favorable the current status of the antecedent) can be computed through the following three steps:

1. For negatively worded statements pertaining to the antecedent, reverse the ratings given by the respondents (i.e., score 7 as 1, 6 as 2, etc.).
2. For each respondent, add the scores on the statements comprising the antecedent and divide the total by the number of statements.
3. Add the scores obtained in step 2 across all respondents and divide the total by the number of respondents.

A final note on the instruments included in appendix B: Because we only recently developed these instruments and have used them in just the latest phase of our research, they have not been subjected to the same degree of testing and refining as our SERVQUAL instrument included in appendix A. We intend to further refine our instruments and procedures for measuring the internal gaps and their antecedents as we use them in future studies.

Exhibit B–1 Instrument to Measure Gaps 1 Through 4

PART I

Directions: This portion of the survey deals with how you think your customers feel about a _____ company that, in their view, delivers excellent quality of service. Please indicate the extent to which your customers feel that excellent _____ companies would possess the feature described by each statement. If your customers are likely to feel a feature is *not at all essential* for excellent _____ companies, circle the number 1. If your customers are likely to feel a feature is *absolutely essential*, circle 7. If your customers' feelings are likely to be less strong, circle one of the numbers in the middle. Remember, there are no right or wrong answers—we are interested in what you think your customers' feelings are regarding _____ companies that would deliver excellent quality of service.

		Our Customers Would Strongly Disagree						Our Customers Would Strongly Agree
1.	Excellent _____ companies will have modern-looking equipment.	1	2	3	4	5	6	7
2.	The physical facilities at excellent _____ companies will be visually appealing.	1	2	3	4	5	6	7
3.	Employees at excellent _____ companies will be neat-appearing.	1	2	3	4	5	6	7
4.	Materials associated with the service (such as pamphlets or statements) will be visually appealing in an excellent _____ company.	1	2	3	4	5	6	7
5.	When excellent _____ companies promise to do something by a certain time, they will do so.	1	2	3	4	5	6	7
6.	When a customer has a problem, excellent _____ companies will show a sincere interest in solving it.	1	2	3	4	5	6	7
7.	Excellent _____ companies will perform the service right the first time.	1	2	3	4	5	6	7
8.	Excellent _____ companies will provide their services at the time they promise to do so.	1	2	3	4	5	6	7

	Our Customers Would Strongly Disagree					Our Customers Would Strongly Agree	
9. Excellent _____ companies will insist on error-free records.	1	2	3	4	5	6	7
10. Employees in excellent _____ companies will tell customers exactly when services will be performed.	1	2	3	4	5	6	7
11. Employees in excellent _____ companies will give prompt service to customers.	1	2	3	4	5	6	7
12. Employees in excellent _____ companies will always be willing to help customers.	1	2	3	4	5	6	7
13. Employees in excellent _____ companies will never be too busy to respond to customers' requests.	1	2	3	4	5	6	7
14. The behavior of employees in excellent _____ companies will instill confidence in customers.	1	2	3	4	5	6	7
15. Customers of excellent _____ companies will feel safe in their transactions.	1	2	3	4	5	6	7
16. Employees in excellent _____ companies will be consistently courteous with customers.	1	2	3	4	5	6	7

(*Continued*)

	Our Customers Would Strongly Disagree					Our Customers Would Strongly Agree
17. Employees in excellent _____ companies will have the knowledge to answer customers' questions.	1	2	3	4	5	6	7
18. Excellent _____ companies will give customerss individual attention.	1	2	3	4	5	6	7
19. Excellent _____ companies will have operating hours convenient to all their customers.	1	2	3	4	5	6	7
20. Excellent _____ companies will have employees who give customers personal attention.	1	2	3	4	5	6	7
21. Excellent _____ companies will have the customer's best interests at heart.	1	2	3	4	5	6	7
22. The employees of excellent _____ companies will understand the specific needs of their customers.	1	2	3	4	5	6	7

PART II

Directions: Listed below are five features pertaining to _____ companies and the services they offer. We would like to know how important each of these features is to *your customers* when they evaluate a _____ company's quality of service. Please allocate a total of 100 points among the five features *according to how important each feature is to your customers*—the more important a feature is likely to be to your customers, the more points you should allocate to it. Please ensure that the points you allocate to the five features add up to 100.

1. The appearance of the _____ company's physical facilities, equipment, personnel, and communication materials.   _____ points

2. The _____ company's ability to perform the promised service dependably and accurately.   _____ points

3. The _____ company's willingness to help customers and provide prompt service.   _____ points

4. The knowledge and courtesy of the company's employees and their ability to convey trust and confidence.   _____ points

5. The caring, individualized attention the _____ company provides its customers.   _____ points

TOTAL points allocated   **100**   **points**

Which *one* feature among the above five is likely to be *most important* to your customers? (please enter the feature's number)   _____

Which feature is likely to be *second* most important to your customers?   _____

Which feature is likely to be *least important* to your customers?   _____

Directions: Performance standards in companies can be **formal**—written, explicit, and communicated to employees. They can also be **informal**—verbal, implicit, and assumed to be understood by employees. For each of the following features, circle the number that best describes the extent to which performance standards are formalized in your company. If there are no standards in your company, check the appropriate box.

	Informal Standards					Formal Standards		No Standards Exist
1. The appearance of the company's physical facilities, equipment, personnel, and communication materials.	1	2	3	4	5	6	7	[ ]

(*Continued*)

	Informal Standards							No Standards Exist
2. The ability of the company to perform the promised service dependably and accurately.	1	2	3	4	5	6	7	[ ]
3. The willingness of the company to help customers and provide prompt service.	1	2	3	4	5	6	7	[ ]
4. The knowledge and courtesy of the company's employees and their ability to convey trust and confidence.	1	2	3	4	5	6	7	[ ]
5. The caring, individualized attention the company provides its customers.	1	2	3	4	5	6	7	[ ]

Directions: Listed below are the same five features. Employees and units sometimes experience difficulty in achieving the standards established for them. For each feature below, circle the number that best represents the degree to which your company and its employees are able to meet the performance standards established. Remember, there are no right or wrong answers—we need your candid assessments for this question to be helpful.

	Unable to Meet Standards Consistently					Able to Meet Standards Consistently		No Standards Exist
1. The appearance of the company's physical facilities, equipment, personnel, and communication materials.	1	2	3	4	5	6	7	[ ]
2. The ability of the company to perform the promised service dependably and accurately.	1	2	3	4	5	6	7	[ ]
3. The willingness of the company to help customers and provide prompt service.	1	2	3	4	5	6	7	[ ]
4. The knowledge and courtesy of the company's employees and their ability to convey trust and confidence.	1	2	3	4	5	6	7	[ ]
5. The caring, individualized attention the company provides its customers.	1	2	3	4	5	6	7	[ ]

Directions: Salespeople, advertising, and other company communications often make promises about the level of service a company will deliver. In some organizations, it is not always possible to fulfill these promises. For each feature below, we want to know the extent to which you believe that your company and its employees deliver the level of service promised to customers. Circle the number that best describes your perception.

	Unable to Meet Promises Consistently					Able to Meet Promises Consistently	
1. The appearance of the company's physical facilities, equipment, personnel, and communication materials.	1	2	3	4	5	6	7
2. The ability of the company to perform the promised service dependably and accurately.	1	2	3	4	5	6	7
3. The willingness of the company to help customers and provide prompt service.	1	2	3	4	5	6	7
4. The knowledge and courtesy of the company's employees and their ability to convey trust and confidence.	1	2	3	4	5	6	7
5. The caring, individualized attention the company provides its customers.	1	2	3	4	5	6	7

Exhibit B–2 Statements to Measure Antecedents of Gaps 1 and 2*

Directions: Listed below are a number of statements intended to measure your perceptions about your company and its operations. Please indicate the extent to which you disagree or agree with each statement by circling one of the seven numbers next to each statement. If you strongly disagree circle 1. If you strongly agree, circle 7. If your feelings are not strong, circle one of the numbers in the middle. There are no right or wrong answers. Please tell us honestly how you feel.

		Strongly Disagree						Strongly Agree
1.	We regularly collect information about the needs of our customers.	1	2	3	4	5	6	7
2.	We rarely use marketing research information that is collected about our customers.(−)	1	2	3	4	5	6	7
3.	We regularly collect information about the service-quality expectations of our customers.	1	2	3	4	5	6	7
4.	The managers in our company rarely interact with customers.(−)	1	2	3	4	5	6	7
5.	The customer-contact personnel in our company frequently communicate with management.	1	2	3	4	5	6	7
6.	Managers in our company rarely seek suggestions about serving customers from customer-contact personnel.(−)	1	2	3	4	5	6	7
7.	The managers in our company frequently have face-to-face interactions with customer-contact personnel.	1	2	3	4	5	6	7

(Continued)

	Strongly Disagree						Strongly Agree
8. The primary means of communication in our company between contact personnel and upper-level managers is through memos.(–)	1	2	3	4	5	6	7
9. Our company has too many levels of management between contact personnel and top management.(–)	1	2	3	4	5	6	7
10. Our company does not commit the necessary resources for service quality.(–)	1	2	3	4	5	6	7
11. Our company has internal programs for improving the quality of service to customers.	1	2	3	4	5	6	7
12. In our company, managers who improve quality of service are more likely to be rewarded than other managers.	1	2	3	4	5	6	7
13. Our company emphasizes selling as much as or more than it emphasizes serving customers.(–)	1	2	3	4	5	6	7
14. Our company has a formal process for setting quality of service goals for employees.	1	2	3	4	5	6	7
15. In our company we try to set specific quality of service goals.	1	2	3	4	5	6	7

	Strongly Disagree						Strongly Agree
16. Our company effectively uses automation to achieve consistency in serving customers.	1	2	3	4	5	6	7
17. Programs are in place in our company to improve operating procedures so as to provide consistent service.	1	2	3	4	5	6	7
18. Our company has the necessary capabilities to meet customers' requirements for service.	1	2	3	4	5	6	7
19. If we gave our customers the level of service they really want, we would go broke.($-$)	1	2	3	4	5	6	7
20. Our company has the operating systems to deliver the level of service customers demand.	1	2	3	4	5	6	7

* Statements with a ($-$) sign at the end are negatively worded and therefore should be reverse-scored (i.e., a rating of 7 should be scored as 1, 6 as 2, 5 as 3, and so on).

Exhibit B–3 Statements to Measure Antecedents of Gaps 3 and 4*

Directions: Listed below are a number of statements intended to measure your perceptions about your company and its operations. Please indicate the extent to which you disagree or agree with each statement by circling one of the seven numbers next to each statement. If you strongly disagree, circle 1. If you strongly agree, circle 7. If your feelings are not strong, circle one of the numbers in the middle. There are no right or wrong answers. Please tell us honestly how you feel.

		Strongly Disagree						Strongly Agree
1.	I feel that I am part of a team in my company.	1	2	3	4	5	6	7
2.	Everyone in my company contributes to a team effort in servicing customers.	1	2	3	4	5	6	7
3.	I feel a sense of responsibility to help my fellow employees do their jobs well.	1	2	3	4	5	6	7
4.	My fellow employees and I cooperate more often than we compete.	1	2	3	4	5	6	7
5.	I feel that I am an important member of this company.	1	2	3	4	5	6	7
6.	I feel comfortable in my job in the sense that I am able to perform the job well.	1	2	3	4	5	6	7
7.	My company hires people who are qualified to do their jobs.	1	2	3	4	5	6	7
8.	My company gives me the tools and equipment that I need to perform my job well.	1	2	3	4	5	6	7
9.	I spend a lot of time in my job trying to resolve problems over which I have little control.(−)	1	2	3	4	5	6	7
10.	I have the freedom in my job to truly satisfy my customers' needs.	1	2	3	4	5	6	7

	Strongly Disagree						Strongly Agree
11. I sometimes feel a lack of control over my job because too many customers demand service at the same time.(−)	1	2	3	4	5	6	7
12. One of my frustrations on the job is that I sometimes have to depend on other employees in serving my customers.(−)	1	2	3	4	5	6	7
13. My supervisor's appraisal of my job performance includes how well I interact with customers.	1	2	3	4	5	6	7
14. In our company, making a special effort to serve customers well does not result in more pay or recognition.(−)	1	2	3	4	5	6	7
15. In our company, employees who do the best job serving their customers are more likely to be rewarded than other employees.	1	2	3	4	5	6	7
16. The amount of paperwork in my job makes it hard for me to effectively serve my customers.(−)	1	2	3	4	5	6	7
17. The company places so much emphasis on selling to customers that it is difficult to serve customers properly.(−)	1	2	3	4	5	6	7

(Continued)

	Strongly Disagree						Strongly Agree
18. What my customers want me to do and what management wants me to do are usually the same thing.	1	2	3	4	5	6	7
19. My company and I have the same ideas about how my job should be performed.	1	2	3	4	5	6	7
20. I receive a sufficient amount of information from management concerning what I am supposed to do in my job.	1	2	3	4	5	6	7
21. I often feel that I do not understand the services offered by my company.(−)	1	2	3	4	5	6	7
22. I am able to keep up with changes in my company that affect my job.	1	2	3	4	5	6	7
23. I feel that I have not been well trained by my company in how to interact effectively with customers.(−)	1	2	3	4	5	6	7
24. I am not sure which aspects of my job my supervisor will stress most in evaluating my performance.(−)	1	2	3	4	5	6	7
25. The people who develop our advertising consult employees like me about the realism of promises made in the advertising.	1	2	3	4	5	6	7

	Strongly Disagree						Strongly Agree
26. I am often not aware in advance of the promises made in our company's advertising campaigns.(–)	1	2	3	4	5	6	7
27. Employees like me interact with operations people to discuss the level of service the company can deliver to customers.	1	2	3	4	5	6	7
28. Our company's policies on serving customers are consistent in the different offices that service customers.	1	2	3	4	5	6	7
29. Intense competition is creating more pressure inside this company to generate new business.(–)	1	2	3	4	5	6	7
30. Our key competitors make promises they cannot possibly keep in an effort to gain new customers.(–)	1	2	3	4	5	6	7

* Statements with a (–) sign at the end are negatively worded and therefore should be reverse-scored (i.e., a rating of 7 should be scored as 1, 6 as 2, 5 as 3, and so on).

NOTES AND REFERENCES

Chapter 1
SERVICE LEADERSHIP SPELLS PROFITS

1. David Birch, "The Atomization of America," *Inc.*, March 1987, pp. 21–22.
2. James Brian Quinn and Christopher E. Gagnon, "Will Services Follow Manufacturing into Decline?" *Harvard Business Review*, November–December 1986, p. 103.
3. Jay Rosenstein, "Top Consumer Complaint: Account Errors," *American Banker*, November 1, 1988, pp. 1, 14–15.
4. "How Readers Rate Service in U.S.: 'The Animals Are Running the Zoo,' " *Atlanta Journal*, March 1, 1987.
5. "Pul-eeze! Will Somebody Help Me?" *Time*, February 2, 1987, p. 49.
6. Alan L. Otten, "How Medical Advances Often Worsen Illnesses and Even Cause Death," *Wall Street Journal*, July 27, 1988, p. 1.
7. Based on an interview with Lowell Levin published in *Bottom Line*, June 30, 1988, p. 1.
8. Stanley Marcus, "Fire a Buyer and Hire a Seller," *International Trends in Retailing*, Fall 1985, p. 49.
9. James G. Carr, "We Flatties Don't Come Back!" *Pace*, November–December 1982, p. 17.
10. Warren Bennis and Burt Nanus, *Leaders: The Strategies for Taking Charge* (New York: Harper & Row, 1985), p. 92.
11. The inspiration for the phrase "providing a service good enough that people will pay a profit to have it" comes from an *Inc.* magazine interview with retailer Stanley Marcus who was quoting the Dayton family in Minneapolis, founders of the Dayton-Hudson Corporation.
12. As quoted in "Companies That Serve You Best," *Fortune*, December 7, 1987, p. 98.

13. Lecture delivered by Robert Onstead at Texas A&M University, College Station, Texas, October 29, 1985.

14. Speech by Joseph Ellis, Center for Retailing Studies Symposium, San Antonio, Texas, October 2, 1986.

15. Peter F. Drucker, "Leadership: More Doing than Dash," *Wall Street Journal*, January 6, 1988.

16. Leonard L. Berry, "Delivering Excellent Service in Retailing," *Arthur Andersen Retailing Issues Letter*, April 1988.

17. "The Quest for Quality," *The Royal Bank Letter*, November–December 1988.

18. Same as note 5, p. 52.

19. Robert D. Buzzell and Bradley T. Gale, *The PIMS Principles—Linking Strategy to Performance* (New York: Free Press, 1987), p. 7.

20. Stew Leonard, "Love Your Customer," *Newsweek*, June 27, 1988, special advertising supplement.

21. As quoted in "Do You Know Me?" *Business Week*, January 25, 1988, p. 79.

22. Valarie A. Zeithaml, "Consumer Perceptions of Price, Quality, and Value: A Means-End Model and Synthesis of Evidence," *Journal of Marketing*, July 1988, p. 14.

23. Same as note 22, p.11.

24. "Brokerage House Embarks on Journey to Quality Service," *Marketing News*, December 21, 1984, p. 9.

25. John A. Goodman, Ted Marra, and Liz Brigham, "Customer Service: Costly Nuisance or Low-Cost Profit Strategy?" *Journal of Retail Banking*, Fall 1986, p. 12.

26. Raymond J. Larkin, "The History of Quality at American Express," *FYI.*, American Express corporate affairs publication, October 9, 1987, p. 4.

Chapter 2
THE CUSTOMERS' VIEW OF SERVICE QUALITY

1. See, for example, Philip B. Crosby, *Quality Is Free: The Art of Making Quality Certain* (New York: New American Library, 1979); and David A. Garvin, "Quality on the Line," *Harvard Business Review*, September–October 1983, pp. 65–73.

2. Writings focusing on service quality include: Christian Gronroos, *Strategic Management and Marketing in the Service Sector* (Helsingfors: Swedish School of Economics and Business Administration, 1982); Uolevi Lehtinen and Jarmo R. Lehtinen, "Service Quality: A Study of Quality Dimensions," unpublished working paper, Service Management Group OY, Helsinki, Finland, 1982; Robert C. Lewis and Bernard H. Booms, "The Marketing Aspects of Quality," in *Emerging Perspectives on Service Marketing*, ed. L. Berry, L. Shostack, and G. Upah (Chicago: American Marketing Association, 1983), pp.

99–107; W. Earl Sasser, Jr., R. Paul Olsen, and D. Daryl Wychoff, *Management of Service Operations: Text and Cases* (Boston: Allyn and Bacon, 1978).

3. A comprehensive scheme for classifying services has been developed by Christopher H. Lovelock, "Classifying Services to Gain Strategic Marketing Insights," *Journal of Marketing*, Summer 1983, pp. 9–20.

4. Further details concerning the development and testing of the SERVQUAL instrument can be found in A. Parasuraman, Valarie A. Zeithaml, and Leonard L. Berry, "SERVQUAL: A Multiple-Item Scale for Measuring Consumer Perceptions of Service Quality," *Journal of Retailing*, Spring 1988, pp. 12–40.

5. Only unweighted mean SERVQUAL scores are shown in this exhibit. The weighted mean SERVQUAL scores, while more negative than the unweighted mean scores, display a similar pattern for each pair of subgroups shown in the exhibit.

6. Patricia Sellers, "How to Handle Customers' Gripes," *Fortune*, October 24, 1988, pp. 88–100.

7. Same reference as in note 6, p. 89.

8. William R. George and Leonard L. Berry, "Guidelines for Advertising Services," *Business Horizons*, July–August 1981, pp. 52–56; Valarie A. Zeithaml, A. Parasuraman, and Leonard L. Berry, "Problems and Strategies in Services Marketing," *Journal of Marketing*, Spring 1985, pp. 33–46.

Chapter 3
POTENTIAL CAUSES OF SERVICE-QUALITY SHORTFALLS

1. David A. Garvin, "Quality on the Line," *Harvard Business Review*, September–October 1983, p. 68.

2. Quoted in "Beyond Customer Satisfaction through Quality Improvement," *Fortune*, September 26, 1988, special advertising section.

Chapter 4
GAP 1: NOT KNOWING WHAT CUSTOMERS EXPECT

1. As discussed in C. Gronroos, *Strategic Management and Marketing in the Service Sector* (Helsingfors: Swedish School of Economics and Business Administration, 1982).

2. Christopher H. Lovelock, "Why Marketing Management Needs to Be Different for Services," *Marketing of Services* (Chicago: American Marketing Association, 1981), pp. 5–9.

3. Karl Albrecht and Ron Zemke, *Service America! Doing Business in the New Economy* (Homewood, Ill.: Dow Jones-Irwin, 1985), p. 6.

4. Thomas J. Peters and Nancy Austin, *A Passion for Excellence* (New York: Random House, 1985), p. 84.

5. Don Lee Bohl, ed., "Close to the Customer," *An American Management Association Research Report on Consumer Affairs* (New York: American Management Association, 1987).

6. Same as note 4, p. 94.

7. *CNN News*, May 25, 1987.

8. J. Carey, J. Buckley, and J. Smith, "Hospital Hospitality," *Newsweek*, February 11, 1985, p. 78.

9. As discussed in "Customer Perceptions of GE Aerospacce," *Customer Focus*, General Electric Company publication, December 1986.

10. Same as note 5.

11. Same as note 5.

12. Kate Bertrand, "In Service, Perception Counts," *Business Marketing*, April 1989, p. 46.

13. "How American Express Measures Quality of Its Customer Service," *AMA Forum*, March 1982, pp. 29–31.

14. Same as note 4.

15. Same as note 5.

16. Mary J. Rudie and H. B. Wansley, "The Merrill Lynch Quality Program," *Services Marketing in a Changing Environment* (Chicago: American Marketing Association, 1985), p. 9.

17. W. E. Crosby, "American Airlines—A Commitment to Excellence," *Services Marketing in a Changing Environment* (Chicago: American Marketing Association, 1985), p. 12.

18. Lisa McGurrin. "Hillbilly Music in the Frozen Peas at Stew Leonard's," *New England Business*, February 17, 1986, pp. 38–41.

19. Same as note 5.

20. J. Curry, "Service: Retail's No. 1 Problem," *Chain Store Age*, January 1987, p. 20.

21. Same as note 17.

22. David Goyne, "Customer Service in Retailing," presentation at Center for Retailing Studies Fall Conference, Houston, Texas, October 11, 1985.

23. "Weinstock's Tackles the Problem of Service," *Chain Store Age*, January 1987, p. 16.

24. Same as note 4, p. 16.

25. Stephen Koepp, "Make that Sale, Mr. Sam," *Time*, May 18, 1987, pp. 54–55.

26. Same as note 25.

27. As quoted in speech by Richard C. Whiteley, "Creating Customer Focus," The Forum Corporation, Philadelphia, Pennsylvania, June 15, 1988.

28. Same as note 3, p. 145.

29. Mike Sheridan, "J. W. Marriott, Jr., Chairman and President, Marriott Corporation," *Sky*, March 1987, p. 48.

30. Same as note 29.

31. Same as note 4.

32. "McDonald's Tries to Keep Personal Touch," *Bryan-College Station Eagle*, May 28, 1985, p. 7A.

Chapter 5

GAP 2: THE WRONG SERVICE-QUALITY STANDARDS

1. Arnoldo Hax and Nicolas S. Majluf, *Strategic Management: An Integrative Perspective* (Englewood Cliffs, N.J.: Prentice-Hall, 1984), p. 90.

2. "Making Service a Potent Marketing Tool," *Business Week*, June 11, 1984, p. 170.

3. "Boosting Productivity at American Express," October 5, 1981, pp. 62, 66.

4. Thomas J. Peters and Nancy Austin, *A Passion for Excellence* (New York: Random House, 1985), p. 95.

5. "At Du Pont, Everybody Sells," *Sales & Marketing Management*, December 3, 1984, p. 33.

6. Lisa McGurrin, "Hillbilly Music in the Frozen Peas at Stew Leonard's," *New England Business*, February 17, 1986, pp. 38–41.

7. Mike Sheridan, "J. W. Marriott, Jr., Chairman and President, Marriott Corporation," *Sky*, March 1987, p. 48.

8. Leigh Bruce, "British Airways Jolts Staff with a Cultural Revolution," *International Management*, March 1987, p. 36.

9. Same as note 8, p. 37.

10. Same as note 3.

11. W. E. Crosby, "American Airlines—A Commitment to Excellence," *Services Marketing in a Changing Environment* (Chicago: American Marketing Association, 1985), p. 11.

12. Same as note 11, p. 10.

13. J. Ott, "Federal Express Starts 24-hour Weather Forecasting System," *Aviation Week*, February 7, 1987, p. 38.

14. "Customers Come First," *The Economist*, December 6, 1986, p. 79.

15. George Russell, "Where the Customer Is Still King," *Time*, February 2, 1987.

16. As discussed in speech by Walter Brown, vice-president of productivity and staffing, Marshall Field's, "Field's Computes Enriched Customer Service," at 1987 National Retail Marketing Association meeting in New York.

17. Ted Levitt, "Industrialization of Service," *Harvard Business Review*, September–October 1976, pp. 63–74.

18. Same as note 4, p. 78.

19. Don Lee Bohl, ed., "Close to the Customer," *An American Management Association Research Report on Consumer Affairs* (New York: American Management Association, 1987), p. 49.

20. Same as note 16.

21. "Mr. Winchester Orders a Pizza," *Fortune*, November 14, 1986, p. 134.

22. Same as note 15.

23. Same as note 3, p. 62.

24. Same as note 3.

25. Mary J. Rudie and H. B. Wansley, "The Merrill Lynch Quality Program," *Services Marketing in a Changing Environment* (Chicago: American Marketing Association, 1985), p. 9.

26. "Marriott Expands Frequent Travelers Program," *Hotel and Motel Management*, February 2, 1987, p. 93.

27. E. A. Locke, K. N. Shaw, L. M. Saari, and G. P. Latham, "Goal Setting and Task Performance, 1969–1980," *Psychological Bulletin*, no. 1 (1981): pp. 125–52.

28. Same as note 3.

29. Same as note 11, pp. 11–12.

30. Same as note 2.

31. Jeremy Main, "Toward Service Without a Snarl," *Fortune*, March 23, 1981, p. 61.

32. Same as note 3.

Chapter 6

GAP 3: THE SERVICE PERFORMANCE GAP

1. Daniel Yankelovich and John Immerwahr, *Putting the Work Ethic to Work* (New York: Public Agenda Foundation, 1983), p. 1.

2. As discussed in B. Katz and R. Kahn, *The Social Psychology of Organizations* (New York: John Wiley & Sons, 1978).

3. Same as note 2.

4. Bro Uttal, "Companies that Serve You Best," *Fortune*, December 7, 1987, p. 100.

5. "At Du Pont, Everybody Sells," *Sales & Marketing Management*, December 3, 1984, p. 33.

6. Leigh Bruce, "British Airways Jolts Staff with a Cultural Revolution," *International Management*, March 1987, p. 37.

7. J. Carey, J. Buckley, and J. Smith, "Hospital Hospitality," *Newsweek*, February 11, 1985, p. 78.

8. Lisa McGurrin, "Hillbilly Music in the Frozen Peas at Stew Leonard's," *New England Business*, February 17, 1986, pp. 38–41.

9. Same as note 7, p. 38.

10. "CS Close-Up," *Customer Service Management Bulletin*, March 25, 1987, p. 8.

11. Thomas J. Peters and Nancy Austin, *A Passion for Excellence* (New York: Random House, 1985), p. 15.

12. Orville C. Walker, Jr., Gilbert A. Churchill, Jr., and Neil M. Ford, "Motivation and Performance in Industrial Selling: Present Knowledge and Needed Research," *Journal of Marketing Research*, May 1977, pp. 156–68.

13. These issues are discussed in Charles Greene and D. W. Organ, "An Evaluation of Causal Models Linking Perceived Role and Job Satisfaction," *Administrative Science Quarterly*, March 1973, pp. 95–103; and R. L. Kahn, D. M. Wolfe, R. P. Quinn, J. D. Snock, and R. A. Rosenthal, *Organizational Stress* (New York: John Wiley & Sons, 1964).

14. As discussed in Arlie Russell Hochschild, *The Managed Heart: Commercialization of Human Feeling* (Berkeley: University of California Press, 1983).

15. Same as note 12.

16. "Service, Strategy Give Edge to Business Competitors," *Marketing News*, June 20, 1986, p. 5.

17. "Pul-eeze! Will Somebody Help Me?" *Time*, February 2, 1987, p. 49.

18. J. L. Heskett, "Lessons in the Service Sector," *Harvard Business Review*, March–April 1987, p. 118.

19. Same as note 18.

20. Same as note 4, p. 104.

21. Michael Kranish, "Somerville Lumber," *Boston Globe*, June 9, 1987, p. 47.

22. Same as note 4.

23. These issues are discussed in William G. Ouchi, "A Conceptual Framework for the Design of Organizational Control Mechanisms," *Management Science*, September 1979, pp. 833–48; and William G. Ouchi and Mary Ann McGuire, "Organizational Control: Two Functions," *Administrative Science Quarterly*, December 1975, pp. 559–69.

24. Same as note 23.

25. Leonard L. Berry, "Reconciling and Coordinating Selling and Service," *American Banker*, February 12, 1986, pp. 4–5.

26. Same as note 6.

27. R. H. Bork, "Call Him Old-Fashioned," *Forbes*, August 26, 1985, p. 66.

28. Rosabeth M. Kanter, "From the Information Age to the Communication Age," *Management Review*, August 1987, p. 23.

29. Don Lee Bohl, ed., "Close to the Customer," *An American Management As-*

sociation Research Report on Consumer Affairs (New York: American Management Association, 1987), p. 47.

30. A. Parasuraman, "Customer-Oriented Corporate Cultures Are Crucial to Services Marketing Success," *Journal of Services Marketing*, Spring 1987, p. 13.

31. Same as note 11.

32. These issues are discussed in J. H. Geer and E. Maisel, "Evaluating the Effects of the Prediction-Control Confound," *Journal of Personality and Social Psychology*, no. 8 (1972): pp. 314–19; and D. C. Glass and J. E. Singer, *Urban Stress* (New York: Academic Press, 1972).

33. J. R. Averill, "Personal Control over Aversive Stimuli and Its Relationship to Stress," *Psychological Bulletin*, no. 4 (1973): pp. 286–303.

34. As quoted in speech by Larry Wilson, "Leadership Aspects and Reward Systems of Customer Satisfaction," at CTM Customer Satisfaction Conference, Los Angeles, California, March 17, 1989.

35. "McDonald's Tries to Keep Personal Touch," *Bryan-College Station Eagle*, May 28, 1985, p. 7A.

36. Thomas V. Bonoma, "Making Your Strategy Work," *Harvard Business Review*, March–April 1984, p. 76.

37. Same as note 29.

38. "Hot-Line!" The Forum Corporation, Boston, Mass., June 22, 1987.

39. "Management Autonomy Adds to Deli Success at Byerly's," *Progressive Grocer*, June 1984, p. 318.

40. George Russell, "Where the Customer Is Still King," *Time*, February 2, 1987, p. 56.

41. "May the Force Be with You," *Inc.*, July 1987, p. 75.

42. Scott McMurray, "Merrill Honors Quality Circles," *American Banker*, August 23, 1983, p. 23.

43. Same as note 42.

44. "How American Express Measures Quality of Its Customer Service," *AMA Forum*, March 1982, p. 30.

45. George H. Labovitz, "Keeping Your Internal Customers Satisfied," *Wall Street Journal*, July 6, 1987, p. 10.

46. As quoted in speech by David Bowen, "Leadership Aspects and Reward Systems of Customer Satisfaction," at CTM Customer Satisfaction Conference, Los Angeles, California, March 17, 1989.

Chapter 7

GAP 4: WHEN PROMISES DO NOT MATCH DELIVERY

1. William R. George and Leonard L. Berry, "Guidelines for the Advertising of Services," *Business Horizons*, May–June 1981, pp. 52–56.

2. As discussed in Leonard L. Berry, "The Employee as Customer," *Journal of Retail Banking*, March 1981, pp. 33–40; and Christian Gronroos, "Internal Marketing—Theory and Practice," *Services Marketing in a Changing Environment* (Chicago: American Marketing Association, 1985), pp. 41–47.

3. Same as note 1.

4. Leonard L. Berry, Valerie A. Zeithaml, A. Parasuraman, "Quality Counts in Services, Too," *Business Horizons*, May–June 1985, pp. 44–52.

5. Mike Burns, "Jiffy Lube International: Success Proves Too Slippery to Handle," working paper, Duke University, Durham, North Carolina, 1989.

6. Same as note 1.

7. As discussed in A. Parasuraman, Valarie A. Zeithaml, and Leonard L. Berry, "SERVQUAL: A Multiple-Item Scale for Measuring Consumer Perceptions of Service Quality," *Journal of Retailing*, Spring 1988, pp. 12–40; and A. Parasuraman, Leonard L. Berry, and Valarie A. Zeithaml, "An Empirical Test of the Gaps Model of Service Quality," working paper, Texas A&M University, College Station, Texas, 1989.

8. Valarie A. Zeithaml, "Consumer Perceptions of Price, Quality, and Value: A Means-End Model and Synthesis of Evidence," *Journal of Marketing*, July 1988, pp. 2–22.

9. Don Lee Bohl, ed., "Close to the Customer," *An American Management Association Research Report on Consumer Affairs* (New York: American Management Association, 1987), p. 80.

10. Same as note 9.

Chapter 8
GETTING STARTED ON THE SERVICE-QUALITY JOURNEY

1. A. Parasuraman, "Customer-Oriented Corporate Cultures Are Crucial to Services Marketing Success," *The Journal of Services Marketing*, Summer 1987, pp. 39–46.

2. Mimi Lieber, "Managing for Service Excellence in a Turbulent Environment," a speech to an American Marketing Association conference, Boston, Massachusetts, February 25, 1987.

3. As quoted in Leonard L. Berry, "Middle Managers Can Play a Key Role in Improving Service," *American Banker*, September 23, 1987, p. 4.

4. "The Chairman Doesn't Blink," *Quality Progress*, March 1987, p. 23.

5. Daniel Yankelovich and John Immerwahr, *Putting the Work Ethic to Work* (New York: Public Agenda Foundation, 1983), p. 1.

6. Same as note 4.

7. Benjamin Schneider, "Imperatives for the Design of Service Organizations," in *Add Value to Your Service*, proceedings of the American Marketing Association Services Marketing Conference, 1987, p. 97.

8. Leonard L. Berry, David R. Bennett, and Carter W. Brown, *Service Quality—A Profit Strategy for Financial Insttitutions* (Homewood, Ill.: Dow Jones-Irwin, 1989), pp. 122–23.

9. John J. Falzon, "Met Life's Quest for Quality," *Journal of Services Marketing*, Spring 1988, pp. 61–64.

10. Leonard L. Berry, Charles M. Futrell, and Michael R. Bowers, *Bankers Who Sell—Improving Selling Effectiveness in Banking* (Chicago: Bank Marketing Association and Homewood, Ill.: Dow Jones-Irwin, 1985), pp. 42–45.

11. Mortimer R. Feinberg and Aaron Levenstein, "It's Not My Job, Man," *Wall Street Journal*, November 11, 1985.

12. As paraphrased in Robert H. Waterman, Jr., *The Renewal Factor* (New York: Bantam Books, 1987), p. 225.

13. Howard Deutsch and Neil J. Metviner, "Quality in Banking: The Competitive Edge," *Bank Administration*, April 1987.

14. Same as note 13.

15. Chip R. Bell and Ron Zemke, "Do Service Procedures Tie Employees' Hands?" *Personnel Journal*, September 1988, p. 79.

16. Same as note 12, p. 73.

17. Same as note 12, p. 88.

18. As quoted in Bell and Zemke, "Do Services Procedures Tie Employees' Hands?," p. 81.

19. Same as note 13.

20. Peter F. Drucker, "Leadership: More Doing than Dash," *Wall Street Journal*, January 6, 1988.

Chapter 9
SERVICE-QUALITY CHALLENGES FOR THE 1990'S

1. G. Lynn Shostack and Jane Kingman-Brundage, "Service Design and Development," in *Handbook of Services Marketing*, ed. Carole A. Congram and Margaret L. Friedman (New York: ANACOM, in press).

2. G. Lynn Shostack, "Planning the Service Encounter," in *The Service Encounter*, ed. John A. Czepiel, Michael R. Solomon, and Carol F. Surprenant (Lexington, Mass.: Lexington Books, 1985), p. 246.

3. See G. Lynn Shostack, "Designing Services that Deliver," *Harvard Business Review*, January–February 1984, pp. 133–39.

4. William R. George and Barbara E. Gibson, "Blueprinting: A Tool for Managing Quality in Service," a presentation to the Symposium on Quality in Services, Karlstad, Sweden, August 1988.

5. Steve Bergsman, "Valley National Streamlines Loan Processes," *American Banker*, March 15, 1989, pp. 9–10.

6. Leonard L. Berry, "Big Ideas in Services Marketing," *The Journal of Consumer Marketing*, Spring 1986, p. 50.

7. Information supplied by Florida Power & Light company officials James Cartwright and Kathy Scott in telephone interviews on April 26 and 28, 1989.

8. Tom Peters, "Twenty Propositions about Service," a speech to the International Customer Service Association, Phoenix, Arizona, September 20, 1988.

9. "Among Restaurateurs, It's Dog Eat Dog," *Business Week*, January 9, 1989, p. 86.

10. "Where the Jobs Are Is Where the Skills Aren't," *Business Week*, September 19, 1988, p. 105.

11. "Help Wanted," *Business Week*, August 10, 1987, p. 49.

12. Louis S. Richman, "Tomorrow's Jobs: Plentiful, But . . . ," *Fortune*, April 11, 1988, p. 44.

13. Same as note 10, p. 104.

14. Roger Selbert, "The Educational Future," *FutureScan*, September 12, 1988, p. 1.

15. As quoted in "Tomorrow's Jobs," note 12, p. 48.

16. James Poisant, "Disney World's Happy-Employee Secrets," *Boardroom Reports*, October 15, 1987, p. 3.

17. Same as note 12, p. 52.

18. Same as note 11, p. 51.

19. Robin Clapp, "The Magic of Disney," unpublished paper.

20. Tom Peters, "Competitiveness Crusade Begins with Your Gripes," *Chicago Tribune*, March 6, 1989.

21. Adapted from Paul Hawkin, "You Are the Customer, You Are the Company," *Whole Earth Review*, 1986.

22. This paragraph is based on material appearing in note 8. The service-quality statistics appear in the *Deluxe Corporation 1988 Annual Report*.

23. This statistic was supplied by Jeff Jones of the product marketing department at Dunkin' Donuts in a telephone interview on April 28, 1989.

24. Donald K. Clifford, Jr., and Richard E. Cavanaugh, *The Winning Performance—How America's High-Growth Midsize Companies Succeed* (New York: Bantam Books, 1985), p. 66.

25. Leonard L. Berry, "Delivering Excellent Service in Retailing," *Arthur Andersen Retailing Issues Letter*, April 1988, p. 2.

26. Leonard L. Berry, A. Parasuraman, and Valarie A. Zeithaml, "The Service-Quality Puzzle," *Business Horizons*, September–October 1988, p. 43.

Appendix A
SERVQUAL AND ITS APPLICATIONS

1. Details about the procedure used in developing and testing SERVQUAL and empirical evidence of the instrument's reliability and validity can be found in A. Parasuraman, Valarie A. Zeithaml, and Leonard L. Berry, "SERVQUAL: A Multiple-Item Scale for Measuring Consumer Perceptions of Service Quality," *Journal of Retailing*, Spring 1988, pp. 12–40.

INDEX

Lightning Source UK Ltd.
Milton Keynes UK
UKOW03f1850030414

229381UK00001B/59/P